THE OPTIONS ADVANTAGE

GAINING A
TRADING EDGE
OVER THE
MARKETS

DAVID L. CAPLAN

PROBUS PUBLISHING COMPANY
Chicago, Illinois

This publication is designed to provide accurate and authoritative information in regard to the subject matter covered. It is sold with the understanding that the publisher is not engaged in rendering legal, accounting or other professional service.

Authorization to photocopy items for internal or personal use, or the internal or personal use of specific clients, is granted by PROBUS PUBLISHING COMPANY, provided that the U.S. $7.00 per page fee is paid directly to Copyright Clearance Center, 27 Congress Street, Salem, MA 01970, USA. For those organizations that have been granted a photocopy license by CCC, a separate system of payment has been arranged. The fee code for users of the Transactional Reporting Service is 1-55738-214-X/91/$00.00 + $7.00.

Library of Congress Cataloging in Publication Data Available.

ISBN 1-55738-214-X

Printed in the United States of America

BB

5 6 7 8 9 0

Credits
The author wishes to acknowledge the following corporations for granting permission to use the materials listed on the following pages.

FutureSource 955 Parkview Blvd., Lombard, IL 60148 (800-621-2628): pages 4, 5, 24, 45, 48, 52, 53, 64, 65, 72, 73, 78, 83, 84, 90, 91, 93, 96, 97, 100, 116, 117, 145, 146, 148, 150, 176.
CQG P.O. Box 758, Glenwood Springs, CO 81602 (800-525-7082): pages 18, 40, 46, 70, 76, 86, 88.
Com-Tech Software 141 W. Jackson, Suite 1531-A, Chicago, IL: pages 81, 82, 139
Chronometrics page 50
Los Angeles Times page 8
Dow Jones and Company pages 21, 51, 153
Optionomics pages 185–214
CBOT 118, 119, 120

Although we have used our best efforts to provide the most accurate, innovative option trading methods available, we cannot promise your future profitability. This information, compiled from sources believed to be reliable, is not guaranteed. Use it at your own risk. No representation is made that future performance will have any relationship to past results or hypothetized examples, or that any position, strategy, or account is likely to achieve profits. There are substantial risks in all trading. Every trader should read the "Option Disclosure Document" provided by the exchanges and brokerage houses. Anytime an option is sold, there is an unlimited risk of loss, and when an option is purchased, the entire premium is at risk. In addition, transaction costs (commissions and fees) are always at risk. All opinions expressed are current opinions, and are subject to change.

CONTENTS

PREFACE

Since finishing *The Professional Options Trader's Manual* in 1987, I have been continually asked when a new and "updated" version would be available. As I explain in the Introduction, even though the original *Manual is* only four years old, and all of the concepts and theories are current and accurate, the changes in the options market and results of continuous research and trading require important additions.

This book presents the most up-to-date information that can be used as a "fine tuning" mechanism to my original work to improve our chances for success. It is a culmination of the last four years' research and actual "hands-on" trading.

If I had to summarize the two most important things that I have learned these past several years, they would be flexibility and patience. I use flexibility in two ways: 1) Flexibility in not being married to a particular view of the market, but being able to flow with the trend of the market. Listen to what the market is telling you by its actual price action. (Others' interpretations may be right or wrong, and your own views of last month may now be incorrect.) and; 2) Flexibility in your choice of options strategies by not just using one or two strategies that you like just because they were successful in the past. These strategies may be inappropriate for today's market.

For example, in 1984 and 1985, ratio option spreads were my favorite. Options were just being introduced, and quite often there were pricing inefficiencies in out-of-the-money options. This, coupled with a previous bull market in gold, silver, and sugar, provided for very high option premiums in out-of-the-money calls, perfect for ratio spreads. At that time, I wanted to do nothing else but these positions. However, in

1986 they began to disappear as the bull markets subsided and more traders began recognizing the inefficiencies.

In the quieter, trading range markets of 1986 and 1987 neutral option positions became my favorite. These ended in late 1988 when volatility continued to drop steadily. In 1989, option volatility was substantially trailing the futures market volatility, making it inappropriate to sell options. In 1990, with low option volatility and large moves in underlying markets, "free trades" were favored.

What we are doing, therefore, is using *flexibility* in working with what the markets give us, not "forcing" a trade that we may like, but does not fit the current technical pattern in the futures or option pricing levels.

Patience can be summarized by not over-trading, and waiting for the best opportunities. Over-trading tends to put too much pressure on us both emotionally and financially, forcing us into difficult situations if a market temporarily moves against us. Waiting for the best opportunities means that we will not buy a call option just because the market is moving up. As I will show, purchasing an option can lose money even if the market continues to move as expected. I require that the market not only be in a trending mode, but also that option volatility be at favorable levels. This allows us the benefits of options (limited risk, lower cash outlay, etc.,) while not being severely hampered by their negative factors (over-valuation, time decay, etc.).

Again readers will note these articles and reports continue to be the product of my actual, hands-on option trading, which has been my primary profession since futures' options were reintroduced in 1982. There is a lot of "mileage" in this book. Take advantage of it. I have experienced the victories and the defeats, and hopefully will save you the dollars that I had to spend in learning what "not to do."

(If you would like a current copy of the *Opportunities In Options* newsletter containing our most up-to-date research, contact our office C/O O.I.O., P.O. Box 2126, Malibu, CA 90265 or 310-456-9699.)

David L. Caplan
Malibu, California

INTRODUCTION

This is not just another options book! Since I immersed myself in options almost ten years ago, I have purchased and read every book on the subject I could find. In the beginning, there were few others available than the free booklets provided by the various futures exchanges. These books uniformly provided a definition of what an option was, a glossary of option terminology, and a description of basic option strategies. In fact, my "Bible" at the time was *Options As a Strategic Investment* by McMillan, a book that was about ten years old. When I wrote my first book on options several years later, *The Professional Option Trader's Manual*, I could still count the number of books on options on both hands. Even more distressing, these books were still very similar to each other. They were technically correct, clinical discussions of options, providing the necessary definitions, Greek letters, mathematics, and probability distribution graphs. The problem was that after reading and studying these books, and feeling I understood them, I still had no idea how options would help me in my trading. Being no different than most other traders, I was searching for the system, method, or black box that would provide me with some type of lead over others, and the markets. Knowing that most traders lost, made me determined to work harder to succeed. Options appealed to me because there seemed to be very few people that understood them. The typical comment from traders was - "Sure I know options. You buy a call if you want the market to go up, and you buy a put if it's going to go down." However, my investigation of options showed that by combining options of different expiration periods or strike prices, and having the ability to buy or sell options, that there were literally billions of combinations of potential strategies.

Because of the few individuals or books that had any information on options, I felt that this was an overlooked and underutilized trading strategy and, more importantly I felt that with hard work and research I could find the "trading edge" I was searching for. Also, having an aptitude in mathematics and probability, I decided that this was the best way to put my talents to use. After all of my work, study, and research into options, simply buying calls or puts did not appeal to me as having a trading edge. (In fact, as I will discuss in detail, I have found that the odds of buying options are heavily against you, except in three specific instances.) Discussions with other traders still provided me with no hint of how to use options. In fact, it was not until a discussion I had with my former broker, who I had chosen because he was more knowledgeable than any other on option trading, that I began to formulate my strategies. He recommended a ratio spread involving gold options. At first, this trade seemed unappealing, since it involved several positions which would cost me three times as much commission, slippage, etc. Further, it seemed that the main benefit of the trade was that there would be little loss if gold went lower. There was something about the strategy that interested me though. Fortunately, this position was recommended to me on a Friday, and I was able to spend the weekend studying this trade and the gold market in detail. I found that by using the ratio spread that he suggested, but changing the parameters (strike prices and expiration periods) I could formulate a position that would be profitable if gold dropped over $400, if it didn't move at all, or even if it rose over $100 per ounce! Gold was trading at about $425 an ounce at that time, and I determined that my range of profitability was from zero to $530. However, even more importantly, if gold did not rise over $75 in the next month (which it had only done once in history), I would not lose, if I took the precaution of closing out the spread if gold rose above $500 after that first month.

Although quite concerned that I had made a mistake in my calculations, I decided to jump in the water and initiated the position. After all, I was bullish on the gold market and these positions had profit potential of up to $10,000 per position with margins of about 10% of that figure, and best of all, a large range of profitability. Well, there was good news and bad news. First, the bad news, the gold market collapsed. I was wrong on the markets direction. But, the good news was even better. The option strategy had totally protected me from loss. In fact, as I expected from my calculations, I was profiting from these positions even though my prediction of market direction was wrong! I then knew that options was what I was looking for. Although they cannot help you to predict market direction, I found that options still could provide an unbelievable advantage of:

1. Magnifying your gains when you are correct on the market;
2. Providing strategies that can be profitable over a wide range of prices; and
3. Strategies that can sometimes make money when your prediction of market direction is wrong.

In 1987 I presented my findings in *The Professional Option Traders Manual*. On the cover it was described as "The first hands-on trading manual detailing the most effective option strategies that can be used to any traders advantage." I also avoided mathematics, Greek letters, and theoretical discussions of probability, and instead discussed how to use options in trading to get a "trading edge," what type of markets to look for, my favorite strategies, etc.

Although the manual was well received by both the public and the industry, there were two factors that I had failed to consider in my original work. The first was the changing nature of the options markets. As option volatility ranged from extremely low levels to extremely high (sometimes without regard to the volatility in the underlying markets), the use of different strategies was required.

The second factor I failed to take into consideration was insights from the daily use of options over the years—that can only be gained by savoring the victories and stomaching the defeats. Although I was able to relate many of these in my *Opportunities in Options* newsletter, I felt frustrated because I knew that no one read everything, and many times because of lack of time or space limitations, I was not able to relate some important new concepts or ideas. This is the reason for my new *Trading Edge* book.

There are two final notes I would like to mention to my readers. First, even though my book uses mostly examples from options on futures, these strategies can also be applied to equity options. The main differences between future options and equity or stock options is use of margin and exercise as discussed at the end of Chapter 1.

Second, I am including a chapter on basic option trading, because my publisher thought that it could benefit new traders that happen to pick up the book as one of their first. If you're an experienced option trader, skim it quickly as a refresher, or skip it entirely. However, I did not include mathematical formulas, or complicated hypothetical discussions. Computers can do all the math you'll ever need, and there are many good texts that cover these subjects already. However, there are few, if any, books that show how to use all this great theory. Just understanding the mathematics of options without knowing how to use them is like knowing how to build a car, but not being able to drive - you just can't get anywhere!

My past subscribers and readers will recognize some of the material in this book from my previous manual, newsletters, and articles. This is necessary both for maintaining continuity, and due to the fact that there is just so much that is worthwhile that can be said about options. Use this material as a refresher to review these important principles which are the cornerstones of our option trading techniques.

CHAPTER 1

The "Trading Edge" Philosophy

BEYOND "LIMITED RISK," "CHEAP," AND "LEVERAGE"

In numerous seminars I've given on options trading, I have often asked participants the main reason that they have used options in the past. Invariably, more than 90% cite limited risk, cheap, and/or leverage as their primary reasons. While options provide these advantages, the use of options for only these reasons can almost guarantee that you will eventually lose your money.

Limited Risk

There is no question that when purchasing options your risk is absolutely limited to the amount of premium that you paid for the option. You know in advance how much you can lose. However, just knowing how much money you're probably going to lose is not very comforting when your chances of making money are very slim. Buying far out-of-the-money options, purchasing over-valued options, and purchasing options in trading range markets are usually "dead ducks." You have almost no chance of making money.

Cheap

Cheap options are always available. For example, you can purchase an option for $25 on an S&P contract that has a value of close to $200,000. However, when was the last time you bought something just because it was cheap? How many of us have bought a "cheap" old car, piece of equipment, clothes, etc. only to find it costing a lot more money later on when it needed repair. This is exactly the same with options. Buying an option just because it is "cheap" is never a good reason.

Leverage

In the example of the S&P option above, you are obtaining leverage of over 99%. However, if leverage is the only factor that impresses you, lotteries provide an abundance of this. For a $1 investment in a lottery you can win tens of millions of dollars, and your chances are probably just as good as making money as with that $25 option in the S&P contract.

Yes, options are cheap and do provide limited risk, and leverage. However, you should not consider only these reasons for buying them: options should only be bought when premiums are reasonable, and your trading plan indicates the market is likely to make a large move with the potential for big profits.

POPULAR MISCONCEPTIONS ABOUT OPTIONS

Learning how to obtain a "trading edge" over the market with options is similar to improving your golf game. You can't go very far unless you unlearn your old bad habits. With options, popular misconceptions that have been advanced by many books and brokers are responsible for significant losses by many traders. Let's examine five of these misunderstood ideas.

1.   *"If you buy an option and the market goes in your favor you will always profit."*

Wrong. When you purchase an option you pay not only for its intrinsic (actual) value, but for its time value. Each day you hold an option, the time value must drop somewhat. The market must move in your favor enough to offset this decay of time value premium. Even if the market has made a large enough move to make your option profitable, unless you cash the option out at an opportune time it must con-

tinue to a move in your favor. Buying options is like swimming up-
stream against a heavy current; unless you move very fast you'll be
swept away.

As shown in Exhibit 1.1, the S&P 500 had moved over 3,000
points higher in four months (a gain of $15,000 per futures contract).
However, some call options would have provided no profit to the trader
during this period. Even more distressing, a not so well-priced call option, that could have been purchased by many investors because of its
reasonable price, actually lost value, even while the market made new
all-time highs. There are many examples of this in recent trading as
shown in Exhibit 1.2, 1.3, and 1.4.

2.   *"There is big money to be made in selling over-valued options."*

This is another good news-bad news situation. The good news is
that over 80% of the time this statement is correct. You will make
money selling over-valued options. The bad news is that the other 20%
of the time can cost you far in excess of all the profits you've made.
This is because when selling options your profits are strictly limited to
the premium you receive. However, your risk is not. And over time, all
markets make giant, unexpected moves. Over the last several years I've
seen moves in silver equal to $20,000 in a futures contract in one hour;
5,000 ($25,000) point moves in the S&P in one day; moves in bonds of
10 ($10,000) points overnight, etc. Getting caught in one of these moves
without a trading plan can wipe out years of profits.

3.   *"It is easy to find arbitrage spreads to guarantee profits."*

The truism here is that discrepancy in prices sometimes allows
trades to be done with little or no risk, and when done in large quantities, substantial profits can be locked in by these traders. However, for
those interested in arbitrage, you will be competing with firms with capital bases of $100,000,000 or more, employing many full-time analysts,
computer technicians, mathematicians, etc., who use both round-the-
clock and full-time computer analysis of markets in the United States
and around the world at costs of tens to hundreds of thousands of dollars
per month. Additionally, because of the volumes in which they deal,
their trading costs are much lower than the average traders. Finally, they
are able to obtain the fills without the slippage (loss occurring in execut-
ing an order) that others would experience. You have the same chance of
competing against these firms and profiting at arbitrage as you would in
beating Jack Nicklaus in golf or John McEnroe in tennis.

Exhibit 1.1

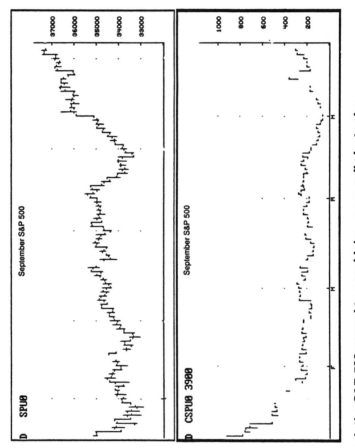

Note: Although the S&P 500 moved to new highs, many calls lost value.

Exhibit 1.2
August Gold 360 Put

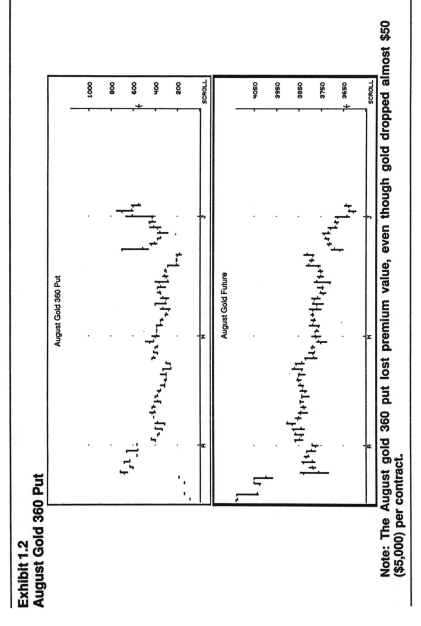

Note: The August gold 360 put lost premium value, even though gold dropped almost $50 ($5,000) per contract.

Exhibit 1.3
September Bond 90 Put

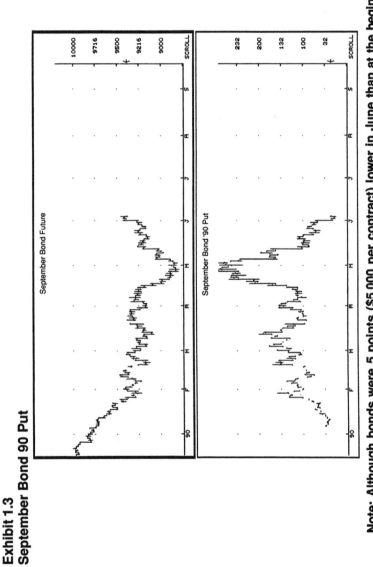

Note: Although bonds were 5 points ($5,000 per contract) lower in June than at the beginning of the year, the September 1990 put lost value.

Exhibit 1.4
June Live Cattle 76 Call

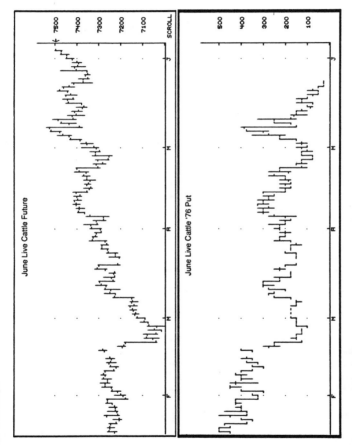

June Live Cattle Future

June Live Cattle '76 Put

Note: In a rising cattle market, the June 76 call still lost value.

Exhibit 1.5

Chess King Kasparov Beats Computer—Twice

It was a battle of two chess champions - one active and outspoken, known to sip tonic water during matches, the other sitting quietly on a desk, taking in a different kind of juice.

World chess champion Gary Kasparov, who has not lost a tournament since 1981, met Deep Thought, the winner of this year's World Computer Chess Championship in Edmonton, Canada, for two games Sunday. The human won both games.

"I'm very happy I could do in both games what I wanted," Kasparov said. "In the first game, with black, I played quietly. In the second game, I tried to crush it in the opening."

The computer retired from the first game after Kasparov's 52nd move and 2 1/2 hours of play. After that victory, Kasparov said: "I expected it. It's a good player but without position and experience."

Playing white in the second game, Kasparov took Deep Thought's queen in move 18. The computer hung on, surrendering after 37 moves and two hours.

"I think the computer needs to be taught something—how to resign," the 26-year old Soviet said.

Kasparov said after the first game he realized early on that he would win when the computer missed some tactical opportunities and was not able to analyze all of the champion's decisions.

"I don't mind who's sitting opposite me," said Kasparov, who live in the Soviet city of Baku, in Azerbaijan. "If a computer should win, of course, I would have to challenge it to protect the human race."

Murray Campbell, who helped create the computer program at Carnegie Mellon University in Pittsburgh, Pa., said it appeared there was a bug in the computer.

"It wasn't looking at the right moves," he said. "It wasn't given a chance to show its best style of play."

Deep Thought, created by five graduate students at Carnegie Mellon, can analyze 700,000 possible positions on the chessboard per second and 5 to 20 moves ahead by each side, as well as discern each move's implications.

Deep Thought evaluates the millions of possible board positions created by each sequence of five moves it imagines. It assigns a numerical value to the positions created by each sequence and moves toward positions with the highest values.

The computer remained in Pittsburgh with a telephone line to relay its moves to a computer terminal in New York.

Kasparov said the computer was "fully aggressive" but that its "mind was too straight and too primitive."

"Chess is much wider than just calculations. It's even wider than logic. You have to use fantasy, intuition and some kind of prediction," Kasparov said.

But he said the computer does have some advantages: "We can lose hope. A computer can't lose hope."

Kasparov captured the world championship in 1985.

Source: *Los Angeles Times*

This is no different than the skills necessary to be a successful options trader. In fact, the chess computers are much more sophisticated than option computer programs.

---

4. *"Computer programs can tell you how to trade options which ones
    to buy and sell, and which strategy to use."*

There are uses for computers in trading options (See Chapter 7)
however, the state of the art in computers is not developed well enough
to analyze all of the various factors that go into option trading. The
computer should be used as a helpful assistant to the trader by evaluat-
ing different types of strategies, crunching numbers, producing what if
scenarios, etc., not as the trader.

5. *"Trading is a zero sum game."*

This often maligned statement is quoted over and over again telling
you for every loser there is a winner. The truth of the matter is that there
are many more losers than winners. This is because all of the costs for
trading must be born by the trader. The brokers, exchanges, all of their
employees, regulatory agencies, are all paid for by you. Add to this the
cost of a computer, publications, and software, and what finally happens
is that for each trading dollar available at the end of the year an average
of 15 to 20 cents is gone for expenses. This means that every year you
must profit by this amount before you break even. This is not an easy
task, and is another reason you should look for only the best positions
that can give you a "trading edge" over the markets.

MY PHILOSOPHY OF TRADING OPTIONS

My objective is to initiate trades that have either favorable risk/reward
ratios or high probabilities of profit. I avoid initiating trades just because
it is my opinion that the market is going up or down, I try to initiate
positions that give some kind of "edge over" the markets through the
characteristics available in options. This means that in buying options I
prefer positions that have the potential for large rewards, while still
keeping risk at manageable levels. When selling options, I seek options
that have high volatility ("overvalued" premium).

I will discuss the methods I use for seeking out the markets with
the best opportunities, how to buy the most favorably priced option that
has the greatest potential of profit, and how to use options to protect
profits, while still being able to build a large position that has a potential
for big rewards by using principles of money management.

In using these techniques, the alert, knowledgeable option trader
should be able to find many opportunities throughout the year that al-

lows him to obtain a "trading edge" over the markets. It may require a little additional work and research; however, this time is very well spent in improving your trading skills.

WHAT IS A "TRADING EDGE"?

A "trading edge" is using options only when you can obtain some "advantage" from them. These advantages can take the form of positions that improve probability of profit, risk/reward or loss control. This also includes strategies that allow for better money management, lessen the need to constantly predict the market or have precise market timing, and allow you to be wrong in your predictions of market direction and sometimes still profit.

This "trading edge" through the use of options has the same objective as other systems or methods that have been designed to give a trader an advantage such as trendline, stochastic, %R, Gann, etc. All are designed to improve your trading and give you a "lead" over others. This is the same way I recommend using options only when they can provide us with a "trading edge" over the markets.

THE ART AND SCIENCE OF TRADING OPTIONS

Trading options is both an art and a science. The "science" is becoming familiar with how an option works, time decay, expiration period, and volatility. The "art" is having an insight on trading options that can only be gained by experience. This includes how to get the best prices for options orders in the different markets, how to best use disparity in option pricing, and which option strategies work the best under various market conditions.

It is my goal to give you as many rules and concepts as possible to improve your knowledge in the area of "science." Unfortunately you must gain your "art" experience on your own in your actual trading. For this reason, it will always be best to trade as small as possible, for as long as possible. There will always be new opportunities in the market to take advantage of . . . unless you've lost your trading capital.

"TRADING EDGE" STRATEGIES CAN BE USED WITH FUTURES, OEX AND STOCK OPTIONS

Although the examples of options strategies in this book are of futures options, the same concepts apply for using these strategies with OEX or stock options. The major differences are in the areas of option exercise and use of margin. Before trading you should obtain a complete updated list of all of the margin and exercise requirements for the options you are considering.

There are several reasons why I prefer trading futures options. First, I like the variety of having over 30 different markets from which to choose. These markets are always in a variety of chart patterns and volatility, allowing me to scan all of the various markets for the most effective option strategies. When it comes to using price disparity between options, I have no bias, whether the market is treasury bonds or soybeans.

Another reason that I favor futures options is the more favorable margin requirements for short options and the ability to receive interest on both investment capital and premium received.

For example, suppose you set up a $10,000 account to be used to obtain premium through selling neutral option positions in the Treasury Bond contract. Let's assume that position was initiated and $5,000 in premium was collected from the sale of these options. Even though this $5,000 in premium value is not yet profits, it can be invested in Treasury Bills to obtain interest along with the initial $10,000 investment. This would allow you to obtain Treasury Bill interest on $15,000, although your original investment was only $10,000. At the end of the year, even if all of your trading broke even, you still would have received Treasury Bill interest on 150% of your initial capital, in addition to your profit opportunities in the markets.

There are also more advantageous rules, recently introduced, in the use of options on futures contracts. A new margining system, the Standard Portfolio Analysis of Risk (SPAN), commenced in 1990 and has provided for a more flexible margining system. SPAN evaluates the overall risk in an entire futures and options portfolio and matches the margin to this risk, applying principles that usually allow for lower margins than in the OEX or stocks.

The OEX options do have one major benefit over the S&P 500 options in the area of liquidity. In May, 1991 the volume on the S&P 500 options was running about 5,000 to 10,000 per day, as compared to the OEX 100 which was about 400,000 and the OEX 500 which was about 80,000. This greatly increased liquidity with Index options provides for more trading opportunities with less slippage (loss due to the difference in the bid/ask spreads).

Since the objective of this book is to learn how to use the characteristics of options to get a "trading edge," knowledge of these differences is important. Traders should also become familiar with the underlying securities, index, or future before initiating positions including the potential volatility of the option or underlying market. However, other than differences inherent in the market underlying the option, and the above differences in the margin and exercise, these option strategies and trading principles can be effectively applied to any market.

CHAPTER 2

BASIC OPTION TRADING CONCEPTS

WHAT IS AN OPTION?

Many chapters, books, volumes, seminars, and tapes have been devoted to complicated discussions of options, trading concepts, formulas, positions, and theories. Unfortunately these materials provide very little in the way of a *concrete plan* on how to use this information for profit.

Too much knowledge can be confusing. A successful real estate investor may not be able to build a house or even draw a plan. However, he may know other more important attributes of the property such as favorable location and marketing techniques. He is only required to use his own innovative talents which may consist of less than 10% of the entire project. However, the creative aspect may be the most important part. Expensive house plans and landscaping ideas may beautify the property; however, if it is in the wrong location or an improper marketing technique is used, it may lose money.

The new investor in options has a similar problem. While there are many books providing accurate descriptions of options, their benefits, varying strategies and mathematical formulas, none have provided a "road map" or plan on how to use this information. Limited risk, price disparity, over and under valuation may sound great, but without a plan on how to use it to profit, where is the opportunity? The following chapters reveal how you can recognize these opportunities and put them to use.

First you need some idea of what an option is, and how it works. Suppose that your next door neighbor has a one acre parcel of land that he is considering selling for $10,000. You feel the property is appreciating and that if you could get the proper permits it would be a great place to build a home and make a profit. However, you want to make sure that you can get the necessary permits and appraise the market in the area before you make the purchase.

In this case you could go to your neighbor and offer him $500 for an "option" or right to buy the property. His answer would probably be . . ."Well, okay, but I will only let you have this right for one year, and then the property will cost you $12,000."

In this transaction you are granted a "call" (right to purchase) option to buy the property for a "premium" (or value) of $500 for a period of one year, "the expiration period," at a price of $12,000—"the strike price." You are the buyer of that option and your neighbor the seller. You can only lose $500, the price you pay for the option; however you have a potential for unlimited gain. If the property goes up in value to $25,000 you would gain $12,500 on your $500 investment when you sold it.

Your neighbor, the option grantor or seller only has $500 to gain, which is the premium he receives; however, if the property goes up in value, he has an unlimited loss potential (even though in this case it would be only of prospective profits).

This is similar to how options work in the futures and stock markets. For example, if silver is currently priced at $4 an ounce, you may decide silver is going up and buy a futures contract. A silver contract consists of 5,000 ounces. Although the contract value is $20,000 (5,000 ounces × $4 an ounce) you must place a deposit of margin (usually 5-10 percent of the contract value) with your brokerage firm which is proof that you can pay your losses if silver goes down. You then make (or lose) $50 for each one cent movement and have unlimited losses or gains.

You can then decide, similar to the option on the land, to instead purchase a silver "call" option. There are several advantages to this. First, no margin is necessary; second, losses are strictly limited to the premium paid for the option; and third, your profit potential is still unlimited.

For example, if you purchase a $4 silver call for $500, if silver goes up during the term of the option to above $4, you can exercise or sell the option to profit. However, if silver fails to move above your option "strike price," or drops in value, similar to the land option, your risk is never more than $500 (Exhibit 2.1).

An option differs from a futures contract or stock in that when you purchase an option, it confers a *right*, but not an *obligation* to purchase (call) or sell (put) the commodity.

There are hundreds of stocks that have options; approximately 50 index options ranging from the OEX 100 to Philadelphia currency options; and over 30 options on futures. The following futures have options that can be traded:

Gold	Corn	Treasury Bonds
Silver	Cotton	Treasury Bills
Copper	Wheat	Treasury Notes
Swiss Franc	Soybeans	Eurodollars
Japanese Yen	Cocoa	S&P 500
British Pound	Orange Juice	NYFE
German Mark	Hogs	Sugar
Canadian Dollar	Cattle	Crude Oil
Nikkei	TOPIX	Japanese Bonds
Platinum	U.S. Dollar	Heating Oil
Gas	Coffee	Pork Bellies

Puts and Calls

There are two types of options: a *call* and a *put* option. The purchaser of a call option has the right to buy the underlying contract at a specified price (the strike price) within a certain time (prior to the option expiration). The seller of a call option has an obligation to sell the underlying contract at the strike price prior to the expiration. A put option gives the option buyer the right to sell the underlying contract at a certain price (the strike price) prior to the expiration time, and conversely obligates the seller to take delivery at this price on or before the expiration date, if the option is exercised.

The option buyer must pay the option seller a certain amount, which is called "option premium." The size of this premium is determined by several factors: the strike price of the option (whether it is "in" or "out" of the money); the time remaining before the option expires; the volatility of the option or the underlying contract; current in-

Exhibit 2.1

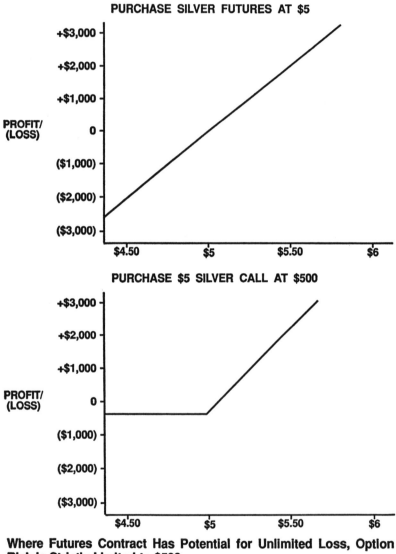

PURCHASE SILVER FUTURES AT $5

PURCHASE $5 SILVER CALL AT $500

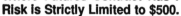

Where Futures Contract Has Potential for Unlimited Loss, Option Risk Is Strictly Limited to $500.

terest rates and, is some cases, supply and demand. (These factors are discussed in more detail later in this chapter.)

The buyer of an option has the opportunity for unlimited profits, with his risk limited to the premium paid for the option. An option seller conversely has unlimited risk, with his profit potential limited to the premium received from the option sale.

All option transactions are opened by either the purchase or sale of a put or call. However, over 98 percent of option transactions are either closed out with an offsetting sale or purchase of the same option, or by letting the option expire worthless, without exercise of the right to take or tender delivery.

For example: gold for delivery in October is priced at $350 on ounce. A gold contract consists of 100 ounces. You decide gold is going up and buy a futures contract. Although the contract value is $35,000, you must place a deposit with your brokerage firm of $1,500 margin to pay losses if gold goes down. You then make (or lose) $100 for each $1 movement and have unlimited losses or gains. Instead, you can decide to purchase a $350 gold call option at $700. There are several advantages to this. First, no margin is necessary; and second, losses are limited to the $700 premium paid for the option. (However, your profit potential is still unlimited.)

HOW AN OPTION WORKS

As shown in Exhibit 2.2, I entered the market at point "A" with *futures contracts*, and was stopped out at "B" with a loss of approximately $750 per contract (not counting potential profit loss of $10,000+). In this instance, I was right on the market, but the need for *precise timing* and *stop loss* was my undoing. Contrast this example with Exhibit 2.3, where I wrongly predicted the market direction, and still made money with a *good option spread*.

At "A", the bullish option spread of long the December 195 call short the 175 put was initiated at $300 credit. In this position, $300 would be collected on a $1,000 margin (30 percent return in 3 months—120 percent annualized) if the market stays in trading range, or moves either slightly lower or higher (below 175 = losses, above 195 = profits of $500 per 100 points). We predicted a trading range market of between 185–192.

We were completely wrong. First, the market dropped to 182, and then took off straight up. We probably would have been stopped out of a

Exhibit 2.2

©1991 CQG, Inc. TQ 20/20

Exhibit 2.3

©1991 CQG, Inc. TQ 20/20

futures position (which would have been at $2,500 loss per position), but our option spread was never at more than a $150 loss. Even though our market prediction was wrong, we were profitable!

Somewhat different than the example of purchasing your next door neighbor's property where you set the strike price (the price at which you would ultimately have the right to purchase the property) and expiration period (the length of time for which you would have this right) by negotiation, the purchaser of a future, stock or OEX option has many different choices. You can purchase options that may expire anywhere from one day to one year. The further away the expiration period (giving more time for your option to become valuable), the more expensive it will be.

You must also decide on the strike price of the option being purchased. If silver is at $4 today, you can purchase silver options, which give you the right to purchase silver at different strike prices of $3, $3.50, $4 . . . all the way up to $7.50. If the market price of silver (the price at which you could sell your silver) is $4, the $3 option is very valuable (and costly) since it would allow you to purchase silver at $1 per ounce under current prices. The $7.50 option will cost much less since it has no actual value currently, but only has what is called "time value." This means that people who purchase the option today know it is currently worthless (who would want to pay $7.50 for silver, when it could be bought anywhere else for $4), but are paying the price because of the chance that silver will go up past the strike price they select sometime in the future.

For example, in May with silver at $4 an ounce, you could purchase a December (the expiration date) at $7.50 (the strike price) silver call for $100 (option premium). This would give you the right to purchase 5,000 ounces of silver (the contract size) at $7.50 any time during the next six months (before the option expires).

If silver stays under $7.50, no one would want to exercise (use) this right, because they could purchase silver elsewhere at under $7.50. However, if silver were to shoot up to say $10 per ounce, this option would become very valuable. In fact it would be worth $2.50 an ounce to the holder of the option ($10 current price less $7.50 strike price = $2.50 profit). Since their option was for 5,000 ounces of silver their option would be worth at least 5,000 x $2.50 = $12,500! Not bad for a $100 investment in six months.

Also important is that the $100 (premium) paid for the option was your entire risk. If someone discovered how to make silver from dirt, and the price of silver fell to $1 or less, your loss could never be more than $100.

Although it would be nice to always buy a cheap $100 option and have the opportunity to make $10,000 or more, buying the cheapest option is not always best. A slightly more expensive option that is "closer-to-the-money" (actual price) provides the best chance to profit. You may have to pay more for this option initially, but it would be more profitable if the market moves as expected. An option with a strike price closer to the actual price of the underlying market is always more expensive. This is because there is a better chance that this option will have value if the market makes a small move, and will be even more profitable in the event of a large move.

For example, with silver trading at $4 an ounce, you may consider purchasing silver call options ranging from $4 to $7.50. Let's assume that the $4.50 call is trading at $500 and the $7.50 call is trading at $100. If silver makes a large move to $10, both option purchasers will be very pleased. The purchaser of the $4.50 silver call will make $5.50 per ounce times the 5000 ounce contract, or $27,500. The purchaser of the $7.50 call will make $2.50 per ounce times 5000 ounces, or $12,500. Although the purchaser of the $7.50 call makes less of a dollar return, his percentage return is more than twice as great! In this case, the trader would have been better off purchasing five $7.50 calls at $100 each (the same cost as one $4.50 silver call) because his total profit would be $62,500 ($35,000 more than the purchaser of one $4.50 call).

Since this once-in-a-lifetime move is unlikely, a more common occurrence would be a move to the $6.50 level. In this case the $7.50 call will be worthless because silver remains $1 under the strike price of the option you own. (Who would want to pay $7.50 for something that could be bought anywhere else for $6.50?) However, the more expensive option, the $4.50 call (which allows you to buy silver $2 per ounce under its current price) is worth $10,000. ($2 per ounce x 5000 ounce contract = $10,000.)

The expiration period, or how long you can hold the option before you lose your right to exercise it is also important. It would be great if you could get an option to purchase silver for $7.50 at any time in the future. But, who would want to sell this kind of option? For every buyer of an option, there must be a seller; therefore, all options have a definite expiration date.

Exhibit 2.4 shows the previous day closing prices for the soybean option contract. It also lists all the strike prices and trading months,

Exhibit 2.4
Barron's/Market Week—Futures Options Closing Prices
Soybeans

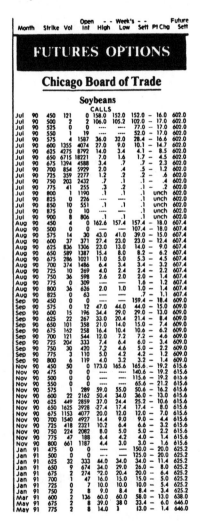

Month	Strike	Vol	Open Int	High	Low	Sett	Pt Chg	Future Sett

FUTURES OPTIONS

Chicago Board of Trade

Soybeans

CALLS

Month	Strike	Vol	Open Int	High	Low	Sett	Pt Chg	Future Sett
Jul	90	450	121	0	158.0	152.0	152.0 − 16.0	602.0
Jul	90	500	2	2	106.0	105.2	102.0 − 17.0	602.0
Jul	90	525	0	0	----	----	77.0 − 17.0	602.0
Jul	90	550	1	19	----	----	52.0 − 17.0	602.0
Jul	90	575	4	1587	36.0	32.0	28.4 − 16.6	602.0
Jul	90	600	1355	4074	27.0	9.0	10.1 − 14.7	602.0
Jul	90	625	4275	8792	14.0	3.4	4.1 − 8.5	602.0
Jul	90	650	6715	18221	7.0	1.6	1.7 − 4.5	602.0
Jul	90	675	1394	4588	3.4	.7	.7 − 2.3	602.0
Jul	90	700	854	5929	2.0	.4	.5 − 1.2	602.0
Jul	90	725	359	2277	1.2	.2	.2 − .6	602.0
Jul	90	750	203	2432	.7	.1	.1 − .4	602.0
Jul	90	775	41	255	.3	.2	.1 − .2	602.0
Jul	90	800	1	1190	.1	.1	.1 unch	602.0
Jul	90	825	0	226	----	----	.1 unch	602.0
Jul	90	850	10	551	.1	.1	.1 unch	602.0
Jul	90	875	0	10	----	----	.1 unch	602.0
Jul	90	900	8	806	.1	.1	.1 unch	602.0
Aug	90	450	4	0	162.6	157.4	157.4 − 18.0	607.4
Aug	90	500	0	0	----	----	107.4 − 18.0	607.4
Aug	90	575	14	30	43.0	41.0	39.0 − 15.0	607.4
Aug	90	600	37	371	27.4	23.0	23.0 − 12.4	607.4
Aug	90	625	836	1306	23.0	13.0	14.0 − 9.0	607.4
Aug	90	650	589	1387	15.4	8.0	8.2 − 6.2	607.4
Aug	90	675	286	1021	11.0	5.3	5.3 − 4.5	607.4
Aug	90	700	374	1486	6.4	3.4	3.4 − 3.2	607.4
Aug	90	725	10	269	4.0	2.4	2.4 − 2.2	607.4
Aug	90	750	36	598	2.6	2.0	2.0 − 1.4	607.4
Aug	90	775	0	309	----	----	1.6 − 1.2	607.4
Aug	90	800	36	626	2.0	1.0	1.0 − 1.4	607.4
Aug	90	825	0	63	----	----	.7 − 1.1	607.4
Sep	90	450	0	0	----	----	159.4 − 18.4	609.0
Sep	90	575	0	12	47.0	44.0	44.0 − 15.0	609.0
Sep	90	600	15	196	34.4	29.0	29.0 − 13.0	609.0
Sep	90	625	22	267	33.0	20.4	21.4 − 8.4	609.0
Sep	90	650	101	358	21.0	14.0	15.0 − 7.4	609.0
Sep	90	675	162	258	16.4	10.4	10.6 − 6.2	609.0
Sep	90	700	121	544	12.0	7.2	7.2 − 4.6	609.0
Sep	90	725	204	333	7.4	6.4	6.0 − 3.4	609.0
Sep	90	750	30	420	7.2	4.6	5.0 − 2.2	609.0
Sep	90	775	3	110	5.0	4.2	4.2 − 1.2	609.0
Sep	90	800	6	119	4.0	3.2	3.2 − 1.4	609.0
Nov	90	450	50	0	173.0	165.6	165.6 − 19.2	615.6
Nov	90	475	0	0	----	----	140.6 − 19.2	615.6
Nov	90	500	0	0	----	----	115.6 − 19.2	615.6
Nov	90	550	0	0	----	----	65.6 − 21.2	615.6
Nov	90	575	1	289	59.0	55.0	50.6 − 16.2	615.6
Nov	90	600	22	2162	50.4	34.0	36.0 − 13.0	615.6
Nov	90	625	449	2859	37.0	24.4	25.2 − 10.6	615.6
Nov	90	650	1625	3928	27.4	17.4	17.4 − 8.0	615.6
Nov	90	675	1153	4077	20.0	12.0	12.0 − 7.0	615.6
Nov	90	700	1540	4927	14.4	9.0	9.0 − 4.4	615.6
Nov	90	725	418	2321	10.2	6.4	6.6 − 3.2	615.6
Nov	90	750	224	2082	8.0	5.0	5.0 − 2.2	615.6
Nov	90	775	47	188	6.4	4.2	4.0 − 1.4	615.6
Nov	90	800	661	1187	4.4	3.0	3.0 − 1.6	615.6
Jan	91	475	0	0	----	----	150.0 − 20.0	625.2
Jan	91	500	0	0	----	----	125.0 − 20.0	625.2
Jan	91	625	32	333	44.0	34.0	34.0 − 11.4	625.2
Jan	91	650	9	674	34.0	29.0	26.0 − 8.0	625.2
Jan	91	675	2	274	?2.0	20.4	20.0 − 6.4	625.2
Jan	91	700	1	47	16.0	15.0	15.0 − 5.0	625.2
Jan	91	725	0	7	10.0	10.0	10.0 − 5.4	625.2
Jan	91	750	2	8	9.0	8.4	8.4 − 3.4	625.2
Mar	91	600	2	136	60.0	60.0	58.0 − 13.0	638.0
May	91	675	2	8	39.0	38 0	33.4 − 6.0	646.0
May	91	775	2	8	14.0	3	13.0 − 1.4	646.0

PUTS

Month	Strike	Vol	Open Int	High	Low	Sett	Pt Chg	Future Sett
Jul	90	500	0	126	----	----	.1 unch	602.0
Jul	90	525	0	865	----	----	.1 unch	602.0
Jul	90	550	175	3792	.3	.2	.2 − .1	602.0
Jul	90	575	857	4170	2.0	1.2	1.4 unch	602.0
Jul	90	600	2751	5940	10.0	5.0	8.2 + 2.0	602.0
Jul	90	625	898	5051	28.0	17.0	27.0 + 8.0	602.0
Jul	90	650	489	2245	49.4	34.0	49.4 + 12.6	602.0
Jul	90	675	50	532	73.5	68.0	73.5 + 14.5	602.0
Jul	90	700	0	40	----	----	98.2 + 15.6	602.0
Jul	90	800	0	0	----	----	198.0 + 17.0	602.0
Jul	90	825	0	0	----	----	223.0 + 17.0	602.0
Jul	90	875	127	0	----	----	273.0 + 17.0	602.0
Jul	90	900	231	3	298.0	282.4	298.0 − 17.0	602.0
Aug	90	500	0	10	----	----	.2 unch	607.4
Aug	90	525	0	149	----	----	.5 + .1	607.4
Aug	90	550	1	218	2.0	1.6	1.6 − .1	607.4
Aug	90	575	95	481	5.4	3.4	5.0 + 1.4	607.4
Aug	90	600	348	1296	16.0	9.0	14.2 + 4.2	607.4
Aug	90	625	95	474	31.0	22.0	30.0 + 8.4	607.4
Aug	90	650	13	76	49.0	44.2	49.0 + 11.0	607.4
Sep	90	500	0	3	----	----	71.0 + 13.4	607.4
Sep	90	525	0	12	----	----	2.0 + .6	609.0
Sep	90	550	1	49	4.6	4.2	4.6 + 1.6	609.0
Sep	90	575	5	49	10.0	9.0	10.0 + 3.0	609.0
Sep	90	600	63	153	20.4	15.0	20.4 + 6.0	609.0
Sep	90	625	4	147	36.0	31.4	36.0 + 9.0	609.0
Sep	90	650	1	31	55.0	50.0	55.0 + 11.0	609.0
Sep	90	675	0	2	----	----	74.0 + 11.4	609.0
Sep	90	700	0	1	----	----	96.0 + 13.0	609.0
Nov	90	500	5	128	----	----	1.0 + .2	615.6
Nov	90	525	1	840	2.1	2.0	2.2 + .4	615.6
Nov	90	550	382	2157	5.0	3.2	5.0 + 1.4	615.6
Nov	90	575	528	2516	10.6	7.4	10.4 + 2.2	615.6
Nov	90	600	406	4124	21.0	14.0	20.4 + 5.2	615.6
Nov	90	625	520	2796	35.0	24.0	34.4 + 8.0	615.6
Nov	90	650	107	1525	52.0	38.4	50.0 + 9.4	615.6
Nov	90	675	515	1352	70.0	64.0	70.0 + 11.4	615.6
Nov	90	700	0	0	----	----	134.6 + 14.6	615.6
Jan	91	575	0	11	----	----	12.0 + 3.2	625.2
Jan	91	600	0	19	----	----	20.0 + 4.0	625.2
Jan	91	625	2	284	29.0	29.0	33.0 + 7.0	625.2
Jan	91	650	552	941	48.0	35.0	48.0 + 9.2	625.2
Jan	91	675	0	600	----	----	66.0 + 11.0	625.2
Mar	91	650	0	2	----	----	44.0 + 8.0	638.0

Call Volume 24,471   Open Int 86,557
Put Volume 9,222   Open Int 43,210
Volume prev Fri. thru Thu.

along with the open interest and weekly volume, for all the individual strike prices. In the case of options on commodities, there are different contract months and expiration dates for all options. For example, in the case of silver, the expiration months are March, May, July, September and December. Unfortunately, many options have different expiration months as shown in Exhibit 2.5. In addition to this confusion, most options expire the month before their stated expiration.

For example, the December 1991 silver option expires on November 8, 1991. Since it is natural to think that a December option should be valid until the end of December, these actual expiration periods can come as an unhappy surprise. For this reason, you should always refer to the chart before purchasing an option.

The more time an option has before expiration, the more costly it will be. Just as close-to-the-money (actual price) strike price's of options are more expensive, so is an option with a longer expiration period because there is a greater chance that it will eventually be valuable.

For example, in May with silver at $4, a one month (July) option with a $5 strike price will cost about $100. A December silver option with the same $5 strike price having six months before expiration would cost about $600. However, in many cases paying more for additional time can make the difference between profit and loss.

In the beginning of 1990, I recommended purchasing May and July 10 cocoa options to my *Opportunities in Options* newsletter subscribers. Several of them complained that the March cocoa calls were much less expensive, and, if the market was going to make a large move that they could buy more of them and make more profit. They were correct in their analysis, but sometimes the market just does not want to cooperate immediately. In this case, having extra time was very important. As shown in Exhibit 2.6, the March cocoa option purchasers would have been very disappointed as the contracts expired in early February under 10 with no profits for them, while the May contract continued to rise providing profits of over $2,000 per option. July cocoa option purchasers paid slightly more for their options (about $150), but were able to hold while the market exploded, with a profit of almost $5,000 per option (Exhibit 2.7).

Therefore, it seems best to buy very long term options that are very close to the actual price of the commodity. Or is it? Unfortunately these options are much more expensive, requiring a large cash outlay as well as more risk. And, from a money management standpoint, you lose

Exhibit 2.5
Options Trading Fact Sheet

OPTION	EXCHANGE	TICK VALUE	TRADING MONTHS	TRADING HOURS (CST)	LAST TRADING DAY (Subject to Change)
FINANCIAL					
TREASURY BONDS	CBT	01= $15.63	ALL	7:20-2:00 5:00 - 8:30	Friday (12:00 CST) which precedes contract month by at least 6 business days
TREASURY NOTES	CBT	01= $15.63	ALL	7:20-2:00 5:00 - 8:30	Friday (12:00 CST) which precedes contract month by at least 6 business days
EURODOLLAR	IMM	01= $25.00	H, M, U, Z	7:20-2:00	First Monday preceding third Wednesday of contract month
S & P 500	CME	05= $25.00	ALL	8:30-3:15	Third Thursday of contract month (Quarterly) Third Friday of contract month (Serial)
NYFE	NYFE	05= $25.00	ALL	8:30-3:15	Third Thursday of contract month (Quarterly) Third Friday of contract month (Serial)
NIKKEI	CME	05= $25.00	ALL	8:00-3:15	Second Friday of contract month (Quarterly) Friday preceding third Saturday of contract month (Serial)
TOPIX	CBT	1/100= ¥2,000	H, M, U, Z	7:00-2:00 5:40-8:15	Second Thursday of month
JAPANESE GOV'T BONDS	CBT	1/2 pt = ¥2,500	H, M, U, Z	7:00-2:00 5:40-8:15	Friday (12:00 CST) of month preceding contract month by at least 6 business days
METALS, CURRENCIES & OILS					
COPPER	CMX	05= $12.50	H, K, N, U, Z	8:25-1:00	Second Friday of month preceding contract month
GOLD	CMX	01= $10.00	ALL	7:20-1:30	Second Friday of month preceding contract month
SILVER	CMX	01= $5.00	H, K, N, U, Z	7:25-1:25	Second Friday of month preceding contract month
PLATINUM	NYMEX	01= $5.00	F, J, N, V	7:00-1:30	Friday preceding first Saturday of contract month
SWISS FRANC DEUTSCHE MARK BRITISH POUND JAPANESE YEN CANADIAN DOLLAR	IMM	01= $12.50	ALL	7:20-2:00	Second Friday preceding third Thursday of contract month
CANADIAN DOLLAR	IMM	01= $10.00	ALL	7:20-2:00	Second Friday preceding third Thursday of contract month
U.S. DOLLAR INDEX	NYCE	01= $25.00	H, M, U, Z	7:20-2:00	Second Friday preceding third Wednesday of contract month
CRUDE OIL HEATING OIL UNLEADED GAS	NYMEX	01= $10.00	ALL	8:45-2:10	Second Friday of month preceding contract month
AGRICULTURE AND LIVESTOCK					
SUGAR	CSC	01= $1.20	H, K, N, V	9:00-12:43	Second Friday of month preceding contract month
ORANGE JUICE	NYCE	01= $1.50	F, H, K, N, U, X	9:15-1:45	First Friday of month preceding contract month
COTTON	NYCE	01= $5.00	H, K, N, V, Z	9:30-2:00	First Friday of month preceding contract month
COCOA	CSC	01=$ 10.00	H, K, N, U, Z	8:30-1:15	First Friday of month preceding contract month
COFFEE	CSC	01= $3.50	H, K, N, U, Z	8:15-12:50	First Friday of month preceding contract month
WHEAT (HARD, RED, WINTER)	KC	1/8= $6.25	H, K, N, U, Z	9:35-1:15	Friday which precedes contract month by at least 10 business days
CORN	CBT	1/8= $6.25	H, K, N, U, Z	9:30-1:15	Friday (12:00 CST) preceding contract month by 6 business days
SOYBEANS	CBT	1/8= $6.25	F, H, K, N, Q, U, X	9:30-1:15	Friday (12:00 CST) preceding contract month by 6 business days
LIVE CATTLE	CME	2.5= $10.00	G, J, M, N, Q, V, Z	9:05-1:00	First Friday of contract month
FEEDER CATTLE	CME	2.5= $10.00	F, H, J, K, Q, U, V, X	9:05-1:00	First Friday of contract month
LIVE HOGS	CME	2.5= $7.50	G, J, M, N, Q, V, Z	9:10-1:00	First Friday of contract month
PORK BELLIES	CME	01= $2.50	G, H, K, N, Q	9:10-1:00	Friday which precedes contract month by at least 3 business days

Courtesy of: "Opportunites in Options" David L. Caplan, Editor
PO Box 2126 Malibu, CA 90265 • (213) 457-3199

Exhibit 2.6

Exhibit 2.7

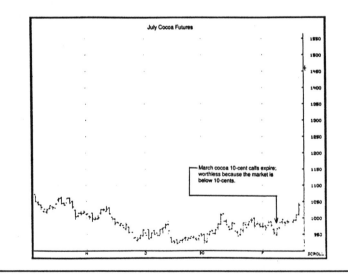

one of the main benefits of options—leverage—if you have to expend large amounts of money in purchasing options.

I have devised a method that combines these sometimes conflicting goals in purchasing options and allows me to purchase what I consider to be the best-priced option—the one having the best chance for success, while still providing enough leverage to produce huge returns if the trade is successful. This method is discussed in detail in Chapter 4.

DETERMINING AN OPTION'S VALUE

The following items determine an options's value: 1) strike price; 2) expiration period; 3) volatility; 4) interest rate; 5) supply and demand.

1) Strike Price and 2) Expiration Period

As discussed above, the strike price of an option is very important in determining an option's value. An option can be "in-the-money" (when the strike price of the option for a call is lower, or for a put, higher than the market price of the underlying future); "at-the-money" (when the strike price of the option is the same as the underlying future); or "out-of-the-money" (when the strike price of the option is higher (call) or lower (put) than the underlying future contract.

An in-the-money option is always the most expensive option, and an out-of-the-money option is always the least expensive. This is because the further out-of-the-money the option is, the less likely it is to have any value at expiration; and the further in-the-money the option is, the more intrinsic value the option has. Intrinsic value is the actual value the option would have if it were to expire today.

For example, an S&P 395 call (allowing you to buy at 39500) would have 500 points of intrinsic value if the S&P was at 40000 at expiration. Only in-the-money options contain intrinsic value. At-the-money and out-of-the-money options contain only time value. This is because if the option expired today, those options would be worthless. Therefore the only value they contain is the potential for a profit in the future. This potential is called "time value." Even in-the-money options contain some time value until close to expiration; however, the closer to the money or the deeper in-the-money an option is, the less time value it contains.

Exhibit 2.8 shows an example of the time decay of an option. Note that the curve begins to accelerate between 30 and 90 days prior to the expiration of the option. This is very important to know when determining whether to buy or sell an option, or which expiration period to use. Also, the time value of in-the-money, at-the-money, and out-of-the-money options decay at different rates, with out-of-the-money options decaying at a greater rate near expiration.

As previously noted, the longer the option has until its expiration the more time value it has. Therefore, a December option to purchase gold at $300 will always have more time premium and value than an October option to purchase gold at $300 (unless we have an inverted market). This is because the additional time gives the option purchaser more of a chance to receive a profit on his transaction.

Although it seems complicated, this is no different than the negotiations entered into when obtaining an option to purchase the house discussed in the preceding chapter. If, for example, the house is worth $100,000 today, there is a good chance that the house could be worth $110,000 in one year. Therefore, a seller would be reluctant to grant you an option to purchase the house at $100,000 in one year.

The negotiations may go something like this:

Seller (option grantor): I'll give you an option to purchase the house in one year at $110,000 (the strike price) if you pay me $5,000 in option money now (premium).

Buyer (option buyer): I prefer to have an option to purchase the house at $100,000 in one year; and am willing to pay you $10,000 for that option.

This type of negotiation (see Exhibit 2.9) occurs before purchasing an option. When an "option" to buy a house is purchased, the "premium" paid for the option is fixed by negotiation between the buyer and seller.

The lower the price (strike price) of this "call option," the more premium the seller will want; and, conversely, the higher the price that is set (e.g., $125,000 for a house that is only worth $100,000 today), the less the option buyer will want to pay, since there is less chance that the property will be worth that price before the option expires.

Similarly, the longer the option period, (time before "expiration"), the more the seller will want, since there is a better chance the option will become valuable before it expires.

The longer time the option is granted for (allowing you to wait to see where the house market or gold market is at that time) the more the option grantor will want for giving you that privilege.

Exhibit 2.8
Time Decay of an Option

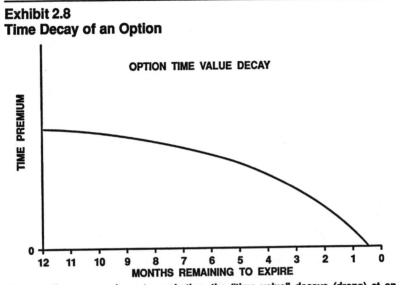

As an option moves closer to expiration, the "time value" decays (drops) at an increasing rate. Decay is especially prevalent in the last months before expiration.

Exhibit 2.9
Option Negotiation

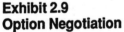

If an option (call) is below the actual price of the market, that option is deemed to be "in-the-money." With gold trading at $375, call options below that figure are in-the-money, such as the 370 call, the 360 call, etc.. If the strike price of an option equals the exact price of the commodity, then it is "at-the-money." An example of this would be if gold had moved up to $380 an ounce, the 380 gold call or put would be "at-the-money."

In the case of a put, it is just the opposite. If the strike price of the put option is above the actual price of the commodity it is "in-the-money." That is because when you are the owner of a put option you have the right to sell the commodity to someone else, so you want that strike price to be as high as possible. With gold trading at $375 per ounce, the 380, 390 and all puts above that are "in-the-money."

An option is "out-of-the-money" when, in the case of the call, the strike price is higher than that of the actual price of the commodity, or in the case of the put, the strike price is lower. In Exhibit 2.10, with gold at $400, all the calls from 410 and above are "out-of-the-money" and all the puts from 390 and below are "out-of-the-money."

When an option is "out-of-the-money" it contains only time value. That is because you would not want to exercise that option currently, since you could buy the commodity cheaper on the open market. For example, if you were granted an option to purchase the house that is currently worth $100,000 today for $110,000 (the strike price), in one year, the only value that option would have is time value. It has no real value today, and its only actual value relies on the fact that at some time in the future it may become more valuable if the price of the house goes up.

This is exactly the same with commodity or stock options. An out-of-the-money option has no real value, only "time value." That continues until the price of the underlying market, in the case of the call, exceeds the strike price of your option, or in the case of a put where the price declines below the strike price of the put you hold. Once this occurs, the option then has real value, "intrinsic value." It has a value of its own, in addition to the time value.

All options contain time value up until the day they expire. However, this time is constantly eroding, causing the time value of the option to decline. This is referred to as "wasting away of the time value." Exhibit 2.11 shows how the time value of the option decays. The time decay wastes away slowly until the option gets about 30 days from expiration. At that time the time value decay accelerates, causing the option

Exhibit 2.10
If the Value of Gold is $400 Today . . .

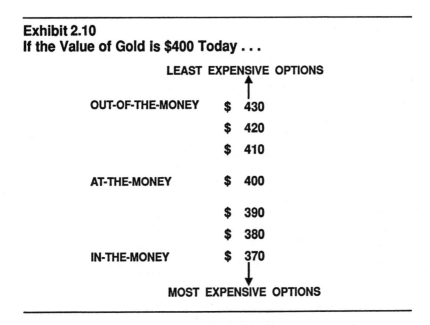

LEAST EXPENSIVE OPTIONS

OUT-OF-THE-MONEY	$ 430
	$ 420
	$ 410
AT-THE-MONEY	$ 400
	$ 390
	$ 380
IN-THE-MONEY	$ 370

MOST EXPENSIVE OPTIONS

Exhibit 2.11
Decay of Time Value

TIME VALUE OF OPTION

180 DAYS   150   120   90   60   30   0

TIME REMAINING BEFORE EXPIRATION OF OPTION

to quickly lose value, as purchasers then think it is unlikely the commodity will gain value.

In the case of the option to buy the house in one year for $110,000, if you paid $10,000 for the option on June 1st and a friend of yours wanted to buy the option from you in two months, if conditions had not changed substantially, you probably could sell it to him for about $9,000 since there is still 10 months left.

Contrast that with the situation where the price of the house had not changed and there were only two weeks before the $10,000 option expired. In that case, few people would be willing to pay anything for the option as it is unlikely that the price would move fast enough to make the option valuable.

It is important to be aware of the time decay of an option. I recommend buying options of at least three months duration, allowing you to hold them so the time value does not decay too quickly; and selling options at least three weeks before expiration if it has not reached your profit objective, so that you do not end up losing all of the premium paid for the option.

These concepts of option strike prices and time value decay are very important in determining the premium of an option that you purchase.

3) Option Volatility

Volatility is the measure of price changes in an option's premium. If a market were to stay in a tight trading range for a long period of time, the option would have low volatility, and therefore little premium, as the market participants see this option as not likely to make a large move. Conversely, if a market were subject to violent price fluctuations, the option would have high volatility and correspondingly high premiums.

Volatility is discussed in more detail in Chapter 3.

4) Interest Rates

Interest rates are also a factor in pricing options. As interest rates increase, option premium decreases; and as interest rates decline, option premiums increase. This is because, from the option buyer's point of view, as interest rates rise an option investment must yield a larger return to keep pace with alternate investments. As rates rise, the option premiums fall to make the investment attractive to prospective purchasers. Therefore, when alternative investments become more attractive to prospective option purchasers, less money is bid for an option premium; premiums will fall, and the potential rate of return on the option rises to reflect the increased opportunity costs. However, of all the factors discussed here, interest rates have the least effect on option pricing.

5) Supply and Demand Factors

Supply and demand factors can help determine option prices to some extent, but are not normally a major factor in a liquid option market. However, in a rapidly trending market (such as crude oil options during the Gulf War), the supply of options to be sold could be lessened since grantors would be reluctant to sell an option with a limited reward if a market is trending strongly. Similarly, in a market that is stable, there could be an oversupply of grantors, thereby lowering the price of an option.

BUYING AND SELLING OPTIONS

On a typical day, buy and sell orders are entered by individuals, brokerage firms, institutions, and floor traders on the floor of the exchange. Let's say that the $6 silver call option closed at $500 the preceding day. The next day when trading opens, prices will be tugged in both directions as investors who think silver is heading higher and would like to buy, pressure the market upward. And investors who are afraid silver's going lower and would like to sell, pressure the market downward.

I may have an order to buy a $6 silver call at a cheaper price than the day's before, for example, at $400. Trader "A", however, may only be willing to pay $350 and Trader "B", $450.

On the other side of the market is Trader "X" who is willing to sell his silver option if he can get $550, Trader "Y" who will sell at $600, and Trader "Z" who wants $650 before she'll sell.

It seems that this silver option cannot be bought or sold, as the highest buy order is $450 and the lowest sell order is $550. This is the normal market scenario, however. If you were to call your broker for a quote on the silver market, he or she would tell you the price of silver is $500 an ounce last price, currently $450 bid, at $550 ask.

So how is this "standoff" broken? There are two ways: 1) new traders' orders entering the market, and 2) negotiations.

As new traders enter the market, they are likely to have different price levels at which they are willing to buy or sell. If a new trader enters the market, for example, to buy at $550, his or her order would be matched with Trader "X" who wants to sell his silver at $500, thereby completing the transaction. Other new traders may come in with "market orders" to buy and sell also. These orders must be filled immediately with the best then-available price. Therefore, new traders constantly entering the market can affect price levels as they place orders to buy and sell.

Here's an example of the second way standoffs are broken—through negotiation: if an option is trading at $450 bid (the highest price at which someone will buy it), at $550 ask (the lowest price at which someone is willing to sell it), what often occurs is that the person with the $450 bid, after not being able to complete his purchase, will eventually move his price up. He is, in effect, stating, "I was trying to get a good deal, but I really want to purchase silver. Is there someone who will meet me half-way and sell?" Similarly, the $550 seller may say, "I would really like to sell my silver today; I think I will lower my price." So they often "meet" in the middle at $500 an ounce.

As in the negotiations to buy and sell most items, such as cars, houses, and antiques, the process between a buyer and seller continues until a mutually-acceptable price has been reached. Most of the time, prices are at an equilibrium or balanced level. This provides both parties a potentially equal chance to profit from a transaction. However, these are not the types of situations for which you are looking. You are only interested in situations where you can have a significant, advantageous "edge."

There are many reasons why these out-of-balance situations might occur. One would be seeing value where others don't. Have you ever purchased an antique, an old car, or a piece of furniture no one else wanted, but after some work or ingenuity, you were able to fix it up and re-sell it for much more than you paid? Have you ever purchased an item a seller had, in your mind, "underpriced" and were able to turn around and quickly sell it for more?

Yes, these are rare cases; prices are usually at equilibrium (balanced) levels. Experience in the markets, however, proves there are many occasions when prices are out-of-line, when there are real price disparities and when there are great opportunities to profit.

OBTAINING FILLS ON OPTION ORDERS AND SPREADS

As mentioned in Chapter 1, trading options is part art and part science. The science in trading options is in knowing how to use volatility, delta, and mathematical probability. However, there is also much that has to be learned in options through actual trading and experience (the "art").

One of the areas that can be learned by only experience is obtaining fills on option orders. The problem with options as compared with futures is that they are much less liquid. Only the most active option contracts, such as crude oil and treasury bonds, have near the volume of a futures contract. Other option contracts, such as heating oil, have about 10% of the daily volume of the underlying contract. This may sound like bad news, but it actually just gets worse. This is because this smaller trading volume and open interest in the options is spread between up to 100 different strike prices. The at-the-money options contain about 10% of the open interest, down to several strike prices away which may have only a few percent.

This makes "fishing" for better prices much more difficult in options than in futures. For example, because of the illiquidity in options, you may see the price of the underlying futures contract change and little or no movement in the price of options, making it difficult or impossible to be filled even at the previous closing price. Further, use of market orders and stops are ill-advised, because of the illiquidity and the substantial slippage that will occur in an active trader's account.

One question that frequently confronts an option spread trader is whether it is advisable to attempt to get filled on a spread individually, or put the entire spread in as one order. For example, if you intend to buy a December 5.50 silver call and sell a 6.00 call, you may find that the spread quote (there are separate brokers that work almost exclusively on filling spread orders alone) is 8 cents bid at 9 cents asked. You would feel reasonably certain of being filled at 8-1/2 cents.

However, if you would like to obtain a better fill, you could put an order in to buy the December silver 550 call at 12 cents and sell the December 600 call at 6 cents (called "legging in"). If the market did have its usual daily swings, you would have a good chance of being filled on at least one side more favorably, if not both. However, there is also the chance of being filled on one side, and watching the other fly away. This type of risk must be assessed, like any other in trading, to determine which method is best for you. I do not recommend that anyone without on-line quote equipment attempt to "leg-in" to option spreads.

The most common spread quotes are for bull and bear spreads and similar common two-sided positions. Anything having more than two positions such as ratio spreads or butterflies are almost impossible to get filled as spreads at reasonable prices. Even conservative traders will have to "leg-in" to these positions at some risk.

I would rate options with a daily volume of under 1,000 as illiquid, from 1,000 to 3,000 as tradable with some difficulty, from 3,000 to 10,000 as liquid and freely tradable, and 10,000 and above as active trading option contracts. Treasury bond options stand in a class of their own with an average daily volume exceeding 50,000 contracts.

The bottom line is that only through experience (the art form of trading) can you determine the best methods of obtaining fills on your option positions or spreads. My years of trading experience in the various option markets are summarized in the tables below. Remember these are the usual bid/ask spread that I have found could be greatly effected by increased or decreased volatility.

Illiquid	**Barely Tradable**
Orange Juice	Wheat
Canadian Dollar	T-Notes
Australian Dollar	Gasoline
Muni-Bond	S&P 500
Soybean Meal	
Soybean Oil	
Heating Oil	
Feeder Cattle	
Cotton	
Cocoa	
Live Hogs	
Pork Bellies	
Lumber	
Copper	
Coffee	
NYSE Index	

Liquid and Freely Tradable

Silver
Japanese Yen
Corn
Soybeans
Swiss Franc
Sugar
Live Cattle
Gold
British Pound
U.S. Dollar Index

Active Trading Options

T-Bonds
Eurodollars
German Mark
Crude Oil
OEX
S&P 100

Exhibit 2.12
Obtaining Fills on Options Spreads

CONTRACT	USUAL BID-ASK (TICKS)- - - - - - - - -				COMMENTS
	SINGLE OPTION: FRONT MONTH	SINGLE OPTION: BACK MONTH	TWO-OPTION SPREAD: FRONT MONTH	TWO-OPTION SPREAD: BACK MONTH	
BRITISH POUND	2-3	3-4	3-4	6-12	With the British pound, buyers can usually get filled a little better than market. Back months are difficult to trade, and participants must be prepared to pay on a hasty exit.
CATTLE	5	10	10	20	On spreads, doing legs individually is usually better.
COPPER	2-5	3-10	3-10	4-20	Most of the action occurs in front month.
CORN	2	3-4	2-4	4-6	Getting filled is usually 2-6 ticks better than the market.
CRUDE OIL	1-3	2-5	2-5	3-9	Buyers can usually get 1 tick better than market. Do spreads as spreads. Prices do not move far out of line because of good volume.
EURO-$	1-2	2-3	4-6	4-6	Do spreads as spreads. If quotes are 2-3 wide, buyers can usually get 1 better than market; with 5-6 wide, it might be possible to get 2 ticks better than market.
GERMAN MARK	2-3	2-5	3-5	4-8	Front months are liquid. Back months are not.
GOLD (COMEX)	2-3	2-5	3-5	4-8	Unlike silver, it is almost always possible to do better than market. Place single-option orders a tick off round numbers to facilitate fills.
HOGS	4-6	6-10	6-10	8-12	Similar to cattle, but harder to trade.

Exhibit 2.12 (Continued)

CONTRACT	USUAL BID-ASK (TICKS)---------				COMMENTS
	SINGLE OPTION: FRONT MONTH	SINGLE OPTION: BACK MONTH	TWO-OPTION SPREAD: FRONT MONTH	TWO-OPTION SPREAD: BACK MONTH	
J-YEN	2-3	4-10	3-5	6-20	Similar to Deutsche Mark, volume has increased, making options easier to trade than in the past.
SILVER (COMEX)	2-4	3-6	3-6	4-8	Difficult to get filled better than market. Back months very difficult to trade; spreads can often be done better individually.
SOYBEANS	4	4-8	6-10	6-12	Similar to corn, we recommend doing spreads as spreads. Orders can usually be done 2-6 ticks better than market.
S&P 500	2-3	4-5	2-4	4-8	Expect 1-2 tick-slippage in and out.
SUGAR	3-6	4-8	5-10	10-15	Similar to Deutsche Mark, volume has increased, making options easier to trade than in the past.
SWISS FRANC	2-4	4-10	4-7	6-20	Back months are difficult. Few market-makers. Less liquid than D-Mark, but front months not a problem, sometimes can get better than market.
TREASURY BOND	1-2	2-4	2-5	3-10	The best option trading market. Fills can be had up to half way across bid-ask.
TREASURY NOTES	2-4	3-6	4-8	5-15	Front month is OK, but back months do not trade much. Tough to get filled better than market. Bond options are superior for short option strategies.

CHAPTER 3

VOLATILITY

WAYS TO USE OPTION VOLATILITY

The most overlooked and underutilized factor by most option traders is the significance of volatility. This includes both the effect of volatility on the premium cost of the option when purchased and of future changes in volatility on the position.

Volatility is simply a mathematical computation of the magnitude of movement in an option. This is based on the activity in the underlying market. If the market is making a rapid move up or down, volatility will rise; in a quiet market, volatility will be low (Exhibit 3.1).

When volatility is relatively low, you should look for option buying strategies as the market is quite likely to make a strong move (Exhibit 3.2); and, when option premium is high, option selling strategies should be considered to take advantage of the relatively over-valued premiums.

Volatility is an important factor in determining the price of an option because all option models depend heavily on the calculation of volatility in determining the "fair market value" of an option. What we are actually saying when we calculate volatility is that the odds are 67% or better that the market will hold within the calculated range over a period of one year.

For example, if gold is trading $500 per ounce and had a volatility of 20%, the probability is that gold will hold a range of $400 to $600

Exhibit 3.1
Market Volatility

TRENDING SEVERELY =
HIGH VOLATILITY
(GREATER EXPECTATION
OF MORE VIOLENT MOVES)

TRADING RANGE=
LOW VOLATILITY
(LITTLE EXPECTATION
OF MARKET-MOVING)

©1991 CQG, Inc. TQ 20/20

Exhibit 3.2
Option Buying Strategies in Low Volatility

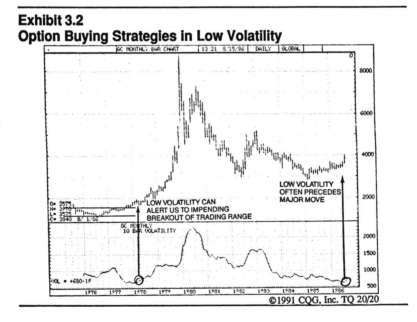

LOW VOLATILITY CAN
ALERT US TO IMPENDING
BREAKOUT OF TRADING RANGE

LOW VOLATILITY
OFTEN PRECEDES
MAJOR MOVE

©1991 CQG, Inc. TQ 20/20

(20% on either side of $500) for a one year period. Based on this, option sellers can calculate the premium they would want to receive for selling various gold puts and calls based on the probability that the strike price would be reached prior to the expiration of the option. If the volatility is high, option sellers would determine that it is more likely that the option price could be reached and ask a higher premium; if volatility is low the option seller would determine that it is unlikely that the option would be exercised and therefore ask less for selling that option.

There are two types of volatility—*historical* and *implied*. Historical volatility is calculated by averaging a past series of prices of options. For example, a trader could use a 90-day price history, a 30-day price history, a 10-day price history, etc. . . . to determine the options "historical volatility." Obviously, each set of calculations result in a different figure for volatility and produce different theoretical (fair value) for the options.

Implied volatility is calculated by using the most current option prices, commodity price level, time to expiration, and interest rate. This method provides a more accurate picture of the current volatility of an option, compared to the historical volatility which is a smoothing of past price action. I use "implied volatility" in my option pricing calculations, and then compare the current numbers to past records of implied volatility (Exhibit 3.3) to determine whether volatility is relatively high or low.

Another overlooked area is the differences in volatility between different months and strike prices of options. When I calculate volatility, I always use strike prices that are nearest to the money, as I feel that this is the most accurate representation of the actual volatility of the option contract. Many times, premiums of out-of-the-money options can be distorted greatly.

For example, in June 1987 silver ratio spreads provided a high probability of profit, because the volatility for the out-of-the-money silver calls were double the volatility of the at-the-money calls. This can lead to significant opportunities. When options approach expiration, volatility for all of the strike prices will tend to equalize. In this instance I purchased the most fairly priced call (near-the-money), and sold the most overvalued calls (out-of-the-money). I could expect the options sold to lose premium faster as the market moved in either direction. Even if the market were to move higher (unless making a straight up vertical move) this spread would have also worked as the nearer-to-the-money option would have gained value faster than the already overpriced out-of-the-money options.

Another overlooked characteristic of volatility is that option volatility tends to drop gradually, then level off. However, volatility increases, at times, can be characterized by very sharp changes in
volatility driving option premium to extremely high levels. These events
occur rarely, but when they do they can be very damaging to those holding short option positions. A recent example was the volatility increase
in many markets at the beginning of the Gulf War. Oil volatility dou-
bled, while other markets such as gold, bonds, and currencies increased
20% or more. Even seemingly unrelated markets such as cattle increased
dramatically.

There are also intraday fluctuations in volatility and premium.
Since implied volatility is based on the closing price of the option, many
times intraday fluctuations in prices will create option volatility that is
much higher than the volatility based on the closing price. (These types
of fluctuations seem to always be of the higher nature. Rarely does option volatility drop any significant degree during a trading day.) Taking

Exhibit 3.3
Volatility Composite Index

	TWO-YEAR RANGE	SIX-MONTH RANGE	MAR	JAN	FEB	VOLA-TILITY TREND	RANKING 1=LOW 10=HIGH
BRITISH POUND	9.6 - 16.7	9.6 - 12.8	12.8	11.1	9.8	UP	8
CATTLE	9.0 - 17.6	9.1 - 14.2	9.1	10.5	9.7	DOWN	1
CORN	14.5 - 28.6	15.4 - 28.6	21.2	17.3	19.8	—	5
COPPER	22.1 - 41.8	22.7 - 34.2	24.5	33.5	27.5	DOWN	3
CRUDE OIL	24.6 - 98.2	29.4 - 98.2	32.4	93.2	63.7	DOWN	2
DEUTSCHE MARK	9.2 - 16.7	9.2 - 12.9	12.9	11.5	10.6	UP	8
EURODOLLAR	10.4 - 28.8	10.4 - 21.2	14.7	13.0	19.9	—	3
GOLD	14.9 - 34.3	14.9 - 34.3	14.9	23.5	18.1	DOWN	1
JAPANESE YEN	8.2 - 17.5	8.2 - 13.6	12.1	12.9	11.3	—	6
S&P 500	15.7 - 33.8	15.7 - 31.8	16.7	22.9	18.2	DOWN	2
SILVER	19.5 - 46.4	19.5 - 34.6	30.1	24.4	34.6	UP	8
SOYBEANS	13.2 - 24.2	13.2 - 24.2	18.3	20.9	18.6	—	5
SUGAR	22.7 - 36.4	25.0 - 35.8	25.0	23.7	22.7	DOWN	2
SWISS FRANC	10.0 - 18.8	10.0 - 13.8	13.2	11.3	10.8	UP	7
TREASURY BOND	8.5 - 16.3	8.5 - 14.2	9.2	14.2	10.1	DOWN	2

advantage of these intraday price swings and distortions in option valuation can provide a trader with significant trading opportunities.

Changes in volatility affect the premium levels in options you are going to purchase, as well as those you have already purchased or sold. A good example of this is in the crude oil and the S&P 500 option market where volatility has ranged between 20% to over 100%. With high volatility, if one were to purchase an out-of-the-money option, you would need a substantial price rise before that option would be profitable at expiration. Both the expense of the purchase price of the option and time value would be working severely against you. However, with volatility at lower levels, this option would not only cost much less but would require a smaller move for the position to be profitable. This is because many times as prices begin to rise volatility also increases, thereby increasing the premium of the option purchased.

The concepts of option volatility, along with the time decay characteristic of options, are the two most important and most overlooked factors in option trading. These concepts can be difficult to learn and use, but the proper use of these option characteristics can result in a "trading-edge" over the markets.

HOW OPTION VOLATILITY CAN ALERT YOU IN ADVANCE TO SIGNIFICANT MARKET MOVES

As discussed above, when option volatility is at low levels, there is a high probability that a large move is about to occur. It seems that when a contract is very quiet, traders seemingly "fall asleep" and don't expect anything to happen. Of course, this is exactly when everything explodes! On the other hand, many times when the market has been very active (volatile) for a period of time, since most traders are already in the market, it is likely to maintain a trading range. However, understanding this concept of volatility is much easier than using it in trading.

The beginning option trader disregards volatility. He determines only that a market is moving in a certain direction, and purchases an option that best fits his view of the market and risk exposure. This trader will lose 100% of the time when the market moves against his desired direction or remains neutral. He will also often lose, even when the market moves in his direction, because of the time decay of the value of the option premium.

The professional option trader will examine the volatility of the option contract and determine whether it's in the high, low or middle of it's historical range. He will then examine a computer evaluation of what the different strike price and months of options will do under various market conditions, and not only choose the option that is the most likely to be profitable, but also determine whether this is an appropriate time to be purchasing options.

For example, call option purchases provided positions with an excellent risk/reward ratio in silver in 1987, and in the grains in 1988. The options had low volatility combined with reliable technical chart patterns which suggested that there was a strong probability of a breakout to the upside (Exhibit 3.4).

The opposite picture was evident in the S&P 500 options in Exhibit 3.5. A trader who would have purchased any out-of-the-money options in the December S&P 500 would have lost money, since the market had very high option volatility (premium) and a short time to expiration. All of the out-of-the-money options, both puts and calls, lost value during this period. Therefore, it didn't matter in this market whether you were bullish or bearish. All buyers of options were wrong, all sellers were right.

Changes in volatility can also occur over short or long periods of time. Treasury bonds had decreased in volatility almost 50% in the beginning of 1987, reflecting a change in traders' views on the market from volatility to stability. On the other hand, Swiss Franc options decreased 30% in volatility in one day after a meeting of the European countries to reevaluate currency rates at which no segment changes were made. Volatility on both puts and calls had increased dramatically during the previous week, and when it was determined that no significant changes were going to occur, in one day, put and call options lost over one-fourth of their value.

Recognizing these principles are not only important in determining the best option strategy to use, but also can alert you to potential changes in the direction of the underlying market.

CONSIDER THE VOLATILITY OF THE UNDERLYING MARKET, AS WELL AS THE OPTIONS

Option traders, like all other investors, are always looking for a deal. In the option trading world this would be the ability to buy a cheap option

Exhibit 3.4
Call Option Purchases (Corn, Silver)

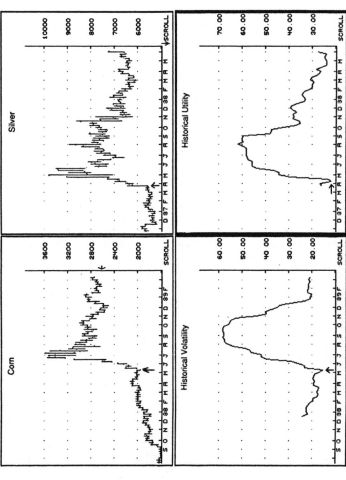

Exhibit 3.5
S&P 500 Options

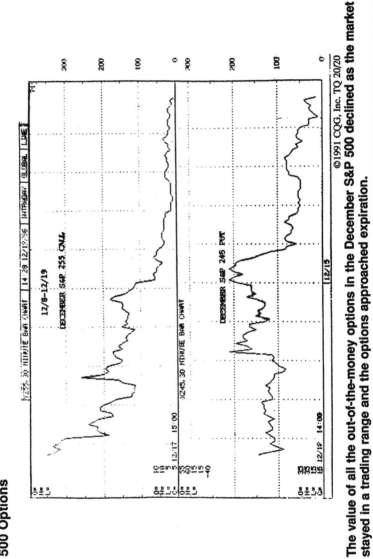

The value of all the out-of-the-money options in the December S&P 500 declined as the market stayed in a trading range and the options approached expiration.

that is likely to appreciate greatly, or sell an expensive option which is likely to deteriorate.

Along with the benefits in option trading, there are complexities. For example, a trend-following trader may decide that Treasury Bonds are in an up-trend; the market has experienced a 30% re-tracement of its current rally, and therefore the most active bond futures contract is purchased with a stop below the last reaction low.

The option trader must not only similarly analyze the market, but also decide what strike price and month of options to use, whether options are to be bought or sold, or whether a combination of options is to be used (a strategy). One of the primary factors option traders use in deciding whether to buy or sell options, or which strategy to use is the volatility of the option market, as this will determine the "premium" paid or received for the trade.

There are times when looking at the underlying market volatility is equally important. The most dramatic example of this occurred in the foreign currencies over the last few years.

From December of 1988 through May 1989 the Swiss Franc declined from 7000 to 5500, a decline of 1500 points in 7 months. During that time option volatility ranged from 12% in the beginning of the move to the 9% level in May and June.

In a similar price move, the Swiss Franc had increased from August through December 1988, from 6500 to 8000, a move of 1500 points in 5 months. However, option volatility differed dramatically from the first half of 1989, at times being twice as high (Exhibit 3.6).

Why did the option volatility vary so much when the underlying market movement was almost the same? In late 1987, the general attitude in the currencies was very bullish as the market was in the throws of a three year bull move. In a bullish market, option premium is almost always higher than bear markets, since small public traders prefer to be long on a market rather than short, thus creating a demand for call options.

This great difference in option volatility means that you also must change your option trading strategies. With volatility at high levels at the end of 1987, selling options premium presented trades with high probabilities of profit. In fact, premium was so high at times, that on days of little activity, option premium shrunk for both puts and calls. However, in 1991, with option premium at levels 50% or more lower, option buying strategies were recommended.

Exhibit 3.6
Volatility (Swiss Franc)

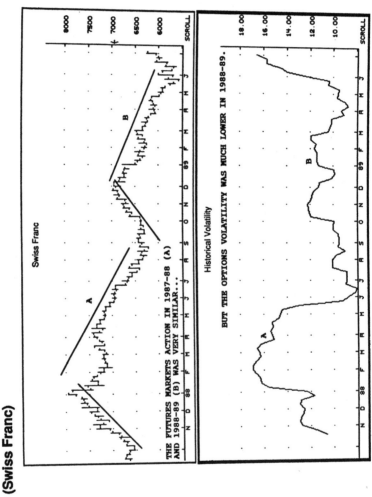

Swiss Franc

THE FUTURES MARKETS ACTION IN 1987–88 (A)
AND 1988–89 (B) WAS VERY SIMILAR...

Historical Volatility

BUT THE OPTIONS VOLATILITY WAS MUCH LOWER IN 1988–89.

In trading options one must learn to be flexible, using what the market gives you to your best advantage. Sticking to one strategy may not be appropriate for current conditions. Changes in volatility levels require the use of different option strategies depending on both the relative level of volatility in the option or underlying market.

USING TRENDS TO YOUR ADVANTAGE

One of the first principles learned when I started trading was "The Trend is your Friend." I have found that to be one of the most important aspects of a trading plan. Attempting to fight the trend, guessing tops or bottoms, trading the correction etc., is probably the biggest cause of losses in the marketplace. Most all traders have done this at one time or another—and paid the price.

Trends are important to option traders not only in determining market direction, but also in determining if option volatility is likely to move higher or lower. Volatility trends similar to price action. Volatility trends are just as reliable and long lasting as price trends, and like price action, when volatility hits low levels and begins to turn up (or high levels and turns down) it can continue to trend for several years.

Volatility trends in options are extremely important in determining the type of trading strategies that are most likely to be successful.

At the beginning of 1988, option volatility in the foreign currencies was extremely high, just coming off historically high levels in some of the foreign currency markets at the end of 1987. Similarly, option volatility was also near the high end of historical levels in the financial markets, in the treasury bond and Euro-dollar option markets. With volatility continually declining during 1988, selling option premium presented trades with high probabilities of profit. This is because the daily shrinkage of time value of option premium was accelerated by the decreasing volatility. In fact, during that period, there were many days and weeks that option premium for both puts and calls moved lower. This type of action, obviously, was very beneficial for *neutral option positions.*

Similarly, the 1982 through 1984 period was excellent for option sellers. The markets had just come off of large movements in the metals and grains, and traders' perceptions were that these conditions would continue. Additionally, options on futures were new, and disparity in pricing occurred more often, since traders were inexperienced in their use and pricing.

Exhibit 3.7
Treasury Bond Options

The above chart of Treasury Bond Option Volatility shows a historical two-year low occurring in the first quarter of 1984. This corre-
sponded to the end of a two-year bear market in Treasury bonds
and the commencement of a major rally. Statistically, there is over
80 percent correlation between extreme volatility changes and
being able to predict market movement.

Exhibit 3.8

Cotton

CALLS

Mth		Strike	Vol.	Open Int.	High	Week's Low	Last	Net Chg.	Futures Close
Oct	91	74.00	21	70	5.60	4.15	4.65	+ 0.62	76.90
Oct	91	75.00	38	116	5.10	3.85	4.00	+ 0.58	76.90
Oct	91	76.00	8	142	5.60	5.60	3.45	+ 0.35	76.90
Oct	91	77.00	21	306	3.55	3.00	2.95	+ 0.40	76.90
Oct	91	78.00	83	185	4.20	2.45	2.50	+ 0.20	76.90
Oct	91	79.00	197	583	2.65	2.00	2.10	+ 0.10	76.90
Oct	91	80.00	137	594	3.30	1.70	1.75	+ 0.05	76.90
Dec	91	71.00	0	462	0.00	0.00	3.44	− 0.40	73.96
Dec	91	72.00	5	732	4.65	4.65	2.96	− 0.44	73.96
Dec	91	73.00	31	276	4.25	3.45	2.60	− 0.46	73.96
Dec	91	74.00	77	557	3.70	3.00	2.25	− 0.28	73.96
Dec	91	75.00	70	1,128	3.25	2.70	1.95	− 0.29	73.96
Dec	91	76.00	17	613	2.70	2.50	1.70	− 0.25	73.96
Dec	91	77.00	8	374	2.40	2.40	1.50	− 0.25	73.96

PUTS

Oct	91	74.00	17	394	1.80	1.15	1.76	− 0.43	76.90
Oct	91	75.00	66	474	2.40	1.65	2.13	− 0.46	76.90
Oct	91	76.00	30	144	2.40	1.70	2.55	− 0.61	76.90
Oct	91	77.00	31	95	3.00	2.25	3.05	− 0.68	76.90
Oct	91	78.00	8	201	4.10	2.55	3.60	− 0.80	76.90
Oct	91	79.00	49	232	4.45	4.05	4.20	− 0.86	76.90
Oct	91	80.00	12	392	4.75	3.60	4.85	− 0.91	76.90
Dec	91	71.00	22	155	2.55	2.25	3.45	− 0.05	73.96
Dec	91	72.00	21	213	2.90	2.90	3.95	+ 0.00	73.96
Dec	91	73.00	10	160	3.50	3.40	4.60	+ 0.05	73.96
Dec	91	74.00	13	302	3.80	3.40	5.25	+ 0.15	73.96
Dec	91	75.00	20	108	4.65	4.15	0.00	+ 0.12	73.96
Dec	91	76.00	2	180	4.50	4.40	0.00	+ 0.17	73.96
Dec	91	77.00	9	42	5.10	4.40	0.00	+ 0.17	73.96

Calls Volume 2,225; Open Int 16,013
Puts Volume 1,116; Open Int 15,535
Volume figures reflect Friday through Thursday.
Open interest figures as of close of business Thursday.
High, Low and Close through Thursday.

Swiss Franc

S-FRANC CALL

JLY	91	620	100	100	—	—	2.25	+	225	.6423
JLY	91	630	160	165	1.59	1.06	1.32	−	28	.6423
JLY	91	635	22	131	1.57	.60	.90	−	34	.6423
JLY	91	640	213	153	1.23	.38	.56	−	37	.6423
JLY	91	645	862	699	.98	.21	.31	−	37	.6423
JLY	91	650	1084	845	.75	.11	.16	−	32	.6423
JLY	91	655	123	353	.54	.05	.08	−	25	.6423
JLY	91	660	781	808	.35	.02	.04	−	18	.6423
JLY	91	665	249	268	.20	.02	.02	−	12	.6423
JLY	91	670	142	606	.13	.02	.01	−	9	.6423
JLY	91	675	75	96	.08	—	CAB	−	7	.6423
JLY	91	680	212	479	.05	—	CAB	−	5	.6423
JLY	91	685	102	229	.01	—	CAB	−	4	.6423
JLY	91	690	6	289	.01	CAB	CAB	−	3	.6423
JLY	91	695		250	—	—	CAB	−	1	.6423
JLY	91	700		200	—	—	CAB	−		.6423
JLY	91	705		249	—	—	CAB	−		.6423
JLY	91	710		55	—	—	CAB	−		.6423
JLY	91	715		546	—	—	CAB	−		.6423
JLY	91	720		177	—	—	CAB	−		.6423
JLY	91	730		20	—	—	CAB	−		.6423
JLY	91	740		65	—	—	CAB	−		.6423
JLY	91	760		34	—	—	CAB	−		.6423
JLY	91	770		50	—	—	CAB	−		.6423
AUG	91	625		1	—	—	2.20	−	17	.6423
AUG	91	635		1	—	—	1.49	−	23	.6423
AUG	91	640	1	18	1.69	1.01	1.20	−	24	.6423
AUG	91	645	2	2	1.41	.69	.96	−	23	.6423
AUG	91	650	34	50	1.27	.42	.77	−	21	.6423
AUG	91	655	16	16	.94	.42	.60	−	19	.6423
AUG	91	660	237	349	.77	.37	.46	−	18	.6423
AUG	91	665	13	21	.46	.36	.35	−	15	.6423
AUG	91	670	12	155	.50	—	.26	−	13	.6423
AUG	91	675		93	—	—	.20	−	12	.6423
AUG	91	680	175	218	.29	.11	.19	−	9	.6423
AUG	91	685		23	—	—	.14	−	8	.6423
AUG	91	690		18	—	—	.08	−	7	.6423
AUG	91	695		9	—	—	.07	−	5	.6423
AUG	91	700		128	—	—	.06	−	3	.6423
AUG	91	705		195	—	—	.05	−	2	.6423
AUG	91	710	10	190	.05	—	.04	−	1	.6423
AUG	91	720		31	—	—	.03	−		.6423
AUG	91	740		10	—	—	CAB	−	1	.6423
SEP	91	625		1	—	—	2.41	−	22	.6423
SEP	91	630		33	—	—	2.08	−	22	.6423
SEP	91	635		117	—	—	1.78	−	22	.6423
SEP	91	640	67	112	2.06	1.30	1.51	−	22	.6423
SEP	91	645	270	268	1.78	1.10	1.26	−	22	.6423
SEP	91	650	77	329	1.56	.93	1.06	−	20	.6423

SEP	91	655	4	10	1.36	.80	.87	−	20	.6423
SEP	91	660	307	467	1.14	.63	.72	−	18	.6423
SEP	91	665	11	30	.69	—	.58	−	17	.6423
SEP	91	670	408	489	.83	.42	.47	−	16	.6423
SEP	91	675		16	—	—	.37	−	15	.6423
SEP	91	680	78	576	.53	.28	.30	−	14	.6423
SEP	91	690	1	513	.36	—	.18	−	11	.6423
SEP	91	700	32	475	.24	—	.10	−	9	.6423
SEP	91	710	20	292	.10	—	.07	−	6	.6423
SEP	91	720	26	222	.06	—	.05	−	3	.6423
SEP	91	730	1	311	.05	—	.02	−	3	.6423
SEP	91	740	2	230	.04	—	.01	−	2	.6423
SEP	91	750		90	—	—	CAB	−	1	.6423
SEP	91	760		29	—	—	CAB	−		.6423
SEP	91	770		68	—	—	CAB	−		.6423
SEP	91	780		142	—	—	CAB	−		.6423
SEP	91	790		195	—	—	CAB	−		.6423
SEP	91	800		44	—	—	CAB	−		.6423
SEP	91	810		79	—	—	CAB	−		.6423
SEP	91	820		42	—	—	CAB	−		.6423
SEP	91	830		47	—	—	CAB	−		.6423
SEP	91	840		42	—	—	CAB	−		.6423
SEP	91	850		3	—	—	CAB	−		.6423
DEC	91	630	1	10	2.86	2.49	2.64	−	15	.6401
DEC	91	650	26	51	1.79	1.60	1.70	−	13	.6401
DEC	91	660	11	32	1.69	—	1.34	−	12	.6401
DEC	91	670	4	184	1.15	—	1.05	−	9	.6401
DEC	91	680	30	142	.83	—	.80	−	9	.6401
DEC	91	690	8	191	.75	—	.62	−	7	.6401
DEC	91	700	9	149	.48	.40	.47	−	5	.6401
DEC	91	710	15	91	.36	—	.35	−	6	.6401
DEC	91	720		51	—	—	.26	−	5	.6401
DEC	91	730		34	—	—	.19	−	4	.6401
DEC	91	740		13	—	—	.14	−	4	.6401
DEC	91	750		3	—	—	.10	−	4	.6401
DEC	91	760		3	—	—	.09	−	1	.6401
DEC	91	770		2	—	—	.07	−	1	.6401
MAR	92	660		20	—	—	1.78	−	7	.6392

S-FRANC PUT

JLY	91	600	5	306	.02	—	.01	−	1	.6423
JLY	91	610	151	151	.01	—	.02	+	2	.6423
JLY	91	620	19	210	.14	—	.03	−	10	.6423
JLY	91	625	18	18	.20	—	.05	−	14	.6423
JLY	91	630	445	506	.33	.10	.09	−	19	.6423
JLY	91	635	878	368	.45	.17	.17	−	25	.6423
JLY	91	640	360	1168	.64	.27	.33	−	28	.6423
JLY	91	645	251	306	.91	.42	.58	−	26	.6423
JLY	91	650	200	762	1.29	.64	.93	−	20	.6423
JLY	91	655	15	199	1.73	.96	1.35	−	13	.6423
JLY	91	660	3	389	1.94	—	1.80	−	7	.6423
JLY	91	665	50	53	2.40	—	2.29	−	1	.6423
JLY	91	670	3	343	2.83	—	2.78	+	3	.6423
JLY	91	675		69	—	—	3.27	+	5	.6423
JLY	91	680		148	—	—	3.77	+	7	.6423
JLY	91	685		32	—	—	4.27	+	6	.6423
JLY	91	690		10	—	—	4.77	+	9	.6423
JLY	91	695	6	27	5.14	—	5.27	+	10	.6423
JLY	91	700		3	—	—	6.77	+	10	.6423
AUG	91	600	1	46	.15	.10	.10	−	5	.6423
AUG	91	610	60	81	.19	—	.18	−	8	.6423
AUG	91	620	42	177	.46	.34	.33	−	11	.6423
AUG	91	625	300	300	—	—	.44	+	14	.6423
AUG	91	630	163	595	.77	—	.58	−	14	.6423
AUG	91	635		3	.92	.73	.76	−	14	.6423
AUG	91	640	40	54	1.16	—	.97	−	14	.6423
AUG	91	645	20	17	1.44	1.11	1.23	−	13	.6423
AUG	91	650	52	44	1.77	—	1.53	−	10	.6423
AUG	91	655		2	—	—	1.86	−	7	.6423
AUG	91	660		75	2.35	—	2.21	−	5	.6423
AUG	91	665		20	—	—	2.61	−	3	.6423
AUG	91	670		100	—	—	3.02	−	41	.6423
AUG	91	675		20	—	—	3.45	+	5	.6423
AUG	91	685		20	—	—	4.36	+	7	.6423
AUG	91	690		3	—	—	4.82	+	7	.6423
SEP	91	600	52	2006	.29	.22	.22	−	7	.6423
SEP	91	610	346	746	.48	—	.37	−	9	.6423
SEP	91	620	435	594	.75	.50	.56	−	12	.6423
SEP	91	625	6	14	.84	—	.71	−	12	.6423
SEP	91	630	351	466	1.08	.72	.87	−	13	.6423
SEP	91	635	27	28	1.27	.93	1.06	−	13	.6423
SEP	91	640	185	419	1.32	1.07	1.28	−	12	.6423
SEP	91	645	260	302	1.79	1.29	1.53	−	12	.6423
SEP	91	650	55	424	2.08	1.50	1.81	−	9	.6423
SEP	91	655	2	5	2.20	—	2.12	−	8	.6423
SEP	91	660	7	460	2.65	—	2.45	−	7	.6423
SEP	91	665		1	—	—	2.81	−	5	.6423

Many weeks both put and call options decline in value, regardless of the direction of the underlying futures market.

One of my favorite positions during this time was *ratio spreads* because the out-of-the-money calls were "over-valued" as compared to the closer-to-the-money calls. By using ratio spreads, I was able to take advantage of this comparative overvaluation.

In 1990, the markets were characterized by not only relatively low option premium but, in fact, option premium that was very low in some markets compared to the daily movement in the futures markets as we discussed above. For example, in 1990 option volatility in the metals, financials and grains was at the low end of historical levels. (Exhibits 3.9 and 3.10) In the currencies, option volatility was neither high nor low historically, but in light of the large daily movement in the futures' markets, option premium was extremely low. Because of this lower volatility the majority of my trades were option purchases with the objective of turning them into "free trades."

In summary, there are two distinct types of trends:

1. Price action; and
2. Volatility

One of the advantages of options is the flexibility of the many different types of strategies. This allows you to pick an option strategy, or design a position to fit the market not visa versa. Flow with these trends in volatility—don't struggle against them.

HOW OPTION VOLATILITY CAN HELP YOU DETERMINE WHICH OPTION STRATEGY TO USE

There are three easy-to-use rules for using volatility:

1. Low Volatility (but beginning to rise)
    Look for a trend change upon a breakout of the six-month trend-line, and then purchase options (*free trades*) or initiate *synthetic futures positions*.
2. High Volatility (but beginning to decline)
    Expect a trading range market which will be excellent for *neutral option positions* because of high option premiums.
3. High Volatility (and market trend almost vertical)
    Look to initiate *ratio option spreads*, as out-of-the-money options will normally be extremely overpriced as compared to close-to-the-money options.

Exhibit 3.9

Exhibit 3.10

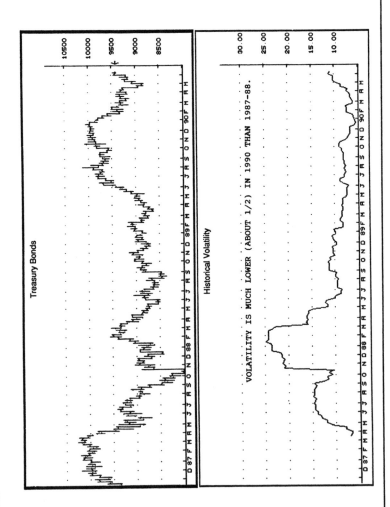

Treasury Bonds

Historical Volatility

VOLATILITY IS MUCH LOWER (ABOUT 1/2) IN 1990 THAN 1987-88.

Knowing these factors of volatility can give you an overwhelming advantage in trading. Being able to sell over-valued, high-priced options that are near expiration can allow you to profit even with an incorrect view in the market. Similarly, being able to purchase low-priced options that will lose little if the market remains stable or moves slightly against you, gives you great holding power. Consideration of these factors can be very important to a trader's pocketbook at the end of the year.

CHAPTER 4

OPTION STRATEGIES

STRATEGIES TO GAIN A TRADING EDGE

Trading options is difficult to learn and even harder to learn to use properly. The advantages of option trading can provide an extra "trading edge," which in many cases can mean the difference between a successful trade and a losing situation. These advantages include:

1. *Limitation of risk* when purchasing options. This allows staying power, the ability to withstand any adverse market move without a margin call no matter how far the market may move against a trader's position. The option buyer can hold his position without being stopped out, or having the potential of unlimited losses, in anticipation of resumption of the market moving in his favor.

2. *The ability to sell* options and profit from the time decay of the option premium. This allows you to sell an out-of-the-money option, by predicting only where the market *isn't* going, and to profit if the market moves in the direction anticipated, stays neutral, or even moves slowly against you.

Option strategies can be designed by combining these two items. When two or more options are combined into a strategy, it is called an option spread. Option spreads can reduce the risk and raise the probability of profit on a trade. Option spread strategies may be used to take advantage of bull, bear, flat or volatile markets. Spreads may vary from a simple vertical spread, with the purchase of a close-to-the-money option and the sale of a further out-of-the-money option, to complex arbitrage spreads which must be adjusted daily to remain "delta neutral."

When determining whether a spread strategy is appropriate, several factors must be present to cause you to go to the time and extra expense (commissions) to employ the spread:

1. *Limitation of risk.* Although risk is already limited by merely purchasing an option, you can further limit risk by employing an option spread strategy. For example, instead of purchasing a December gold 320 call for $2,000 (your risk of loss), purchase a December gold 320 call for $2,000 and sell the December 340 call for $1,000, thereby lowering your risk on this trade to $1,000 (Exhibit 4.1).

2. *Time decay.* The second reason to use option strategies is to be able to benefit from the time decay of the options sold. As noted earlier, many times options will lose value even if the market moves in their favor.

Exhibit 4.1
A Bull Spread vs. Outright Call Buy

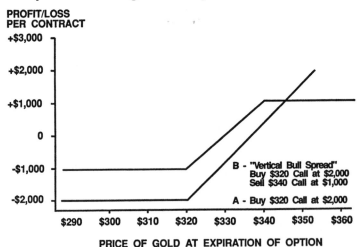

PROFIT/LOSS
PER CONTRACT

B - "Vertical Bull Spread"
Buy $320 Call at $2,000
Sell $340 Call at $1,000

A - Buy $320 Call at $2,000

PRICE OF GOLD AT EXPIRATION OF OPTION

The 320-340 bull spread reduces the risk as well as the profit compared with an outright call buy.

3. *Disparities in option premium levels.* Strategies are also employed to take advantage of disparities in option premiums which occur from time to time. For example, during extended rallies or declines, out-of-the-money options can be overvalued, as the public usually wants to participate in these markets by obtaining great leverage, which can only be found in out-of-the-money options. This drives up the prices of these out-of-the-money options. Spreads formulated by selling these options can then be employed with high probabilities of profit. (These and other important benefits of option strategies are discussed in greater detail in Chapter 6.)

Exhibit 4.32, at the end of this chapter, provides a summary of the most common option strategies and their characteristics. The following positions are those that I use most of the time in my own actual trading that provide me with the most significant advantage ("Trading Edge"):

1. Free Trade (Option Purchase and Later Hedge)
2. Synthetic Futures Position
3. Ratio Spread
4. Neutral Option Position
5. Reverse Ratio Spreads
6. In-The-Money-Debit Spread
7. Calendar Spread

To avoid unnecessary duplication in explaining these strategies, examples use "call" options only. Of course, all of these positions can also be initiated with puts. For example, in discussing a bullish call option ratio spread—(buy a close-to-the-money call - sell two or more out-of-the-money calls)—by substituting the word "put" for call, the position becomes a bearish put option ratio spread.

CHOOSING AND PURCHASING OPTIONS

Indiscriminate option purchasing is one of the biggest causes of losses in trading, since the odds are against the indiscriminate option purchaser because of the "time decay" principles. Therefore, a solid plan is necessary.

The reason most often given for using options (from books, advisors, brokers, and in fact, the Exchange's own pamphlets) is the limited risk factor in purchasing options. Do options truly provide limited risk to the investor? The answer is yes, however this exists only for a limited period of time. (Options always expire at a definite time, and if "rolled," to a further expiration a new premium cost must be paid.) This means not only can you lose money if you are incorrect in your market judgment, you can also lose money when your view of the market is correct. As discussed in Chapter 1, there are many times when a trader who bought options lost money even though the market virtually exploded in his favor. Purchase of the wrong option, or purchasing options at the wrong time will cause this type of loss. Again this is why the correlation of option traders winning or losing is exactly the same as with other traders. Perhaps the option buyers only consolation seems to be with a degree of comfortableness in that they know, in advance, how much they are going to lose.

Three circumstances in which buying options are recommended include, when:

1. The option contains very little time value either by virtue of being close to expiration, and/or close-to-the-money (for short-term moves only).
2. The volatility (premium cost) of the option is at a relatively low level.
3. The trader feels that a substantial market move is imminent.

The trader must also make an appraisal of both the timing and the strength of the move. This does not have to be done with exactness; he must only determine whether a move will occur in a week, month, three months, six months etc., and whether the move will be gradual, or sharp and immediate. This appraisal will greatly effect the month and strike price of the option recommended.

If the market were to make a sharp move, the nearest to expiration option will appreciate the quickest; but it will also lose its value the fastest unless this immediate move occurs.

Let's assume, for example, that on May 4, 1990, we were considering the purchase of a Treasury Bond call option with the June contract at 92-06, the September contract at 92-01, and the December contract at 91-26. The June contract has three days until expiration, the September contract three months until expiration, and the December contract six months until expiration.

If you purchased the June 94 call (approximately 2 points out-of-the-money), a move up of 4 points prior to expiration would cause this option to move from $250 to $2,000, a gain of 8 to 1, while the September and December options would merely double in value. (This can be determined by the use of computers—see Chapter 7.) If you had a very strong feeling that the market was going to move quickly, obviously the leverage and profits would be greatest in using the June options (Exhibit 4.2).

However, the amount of risk that one wants to take is another consideration in purchasing an option. Although the risk is always limited to the amount of premium that you pay for the option, and can be controlled even more by selling the option you buy prior to expiration, generally the closer to-the-money the option is, the more expensive it is, and the more risk it will have. That means that even though the June call discussed above has the potential for the longest quick gains, it will also lose value faster if the market fails to move.

Assume you decide to purchase a 92 bond call in June, September, and December thirty days prior to expiration, and one month later the market is unchanged; the June option will lose about $350, the Septem-

Exhibit 4.2
Purchase Options

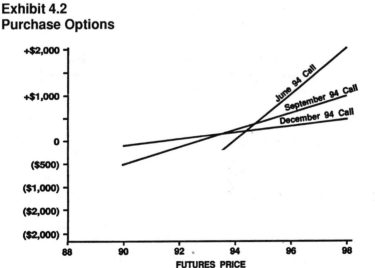

If the market makes a fast move higher, the close-to-expiration June option will gain the most.

ber option will lose $250, and the December option will lose $100. However, if the market were to move up 4 points, the June option would gain almost $4,000 in value, the September option about $2,600 in value, and the December option about $2,000. On a move down of 4 points the June call would lose $500, the September call $350, and the December call $250.

How do you balance all of these conflicting factors of trying to keep risk low, while increasing leverage, and applying sound money management principles? The following specific rules can be used for purchasing options:

1. Never purchase an option with less than 60 days until expiration, unless you expect a very quick, sharp move. Never risk more than $500 per option on this type of purchase, and most important, have a plan of either taking profits on the option at a pre-set level or selling a higher-up option to turn this into a "Free Trade." (We will discuss the "Free Trade" in the next section.) This is to make certain that you do not watch your profits "waste away."

2. Purchase options having between three and six months before expiration.

3. The most difficult factor is determining which strike price to purchase. Two rules are important here:

   a. Never purchase an option more than three strike prices from the money. This is because further out-of-the-money options are unlikely to become profitable.

   b. Look at the risk-reward of purchasing various options. For example, in deciding between the 92 and 94 September call, by comparing the actual cost of the two options, you can determine that it would cost an extra $1,000 for the 92 call, for only an additional $2,000 profit potential (a 2 to 1 risk-reward). However, in deciding between the 94 or 96 September call, there is only a $500 difference between these two calls and therefore a 4 to 1 risk-reward. Use 4 to 1 as your break-point in determining which option to purchase; if the risk-reward is higher than 4 to 1, purchase the closer-to-the-money option; at 4 to 1 or less, purchase the farther-away-from-the-money option.

This principle not only provides for sound money management, but also improves your risk-reward ratio, and allows the purchase of the most fairly valued option. Many times, as in the treasury bond example above, the choice of options to purchase is a very close one, and, in fact, either could be correct. At other times, one option can cost only $25 or $50 more and give you an additional $2,000 or more profit potential. Clearly, in that case, the higher priced option is the correct one to purchase.

PROFIT OBJECTIVES IN OPTION TRADES

An often overlooked subject, when purchasing an option, is that of the profit objective of the trade. Without a plan, a trader can watch an option quickly run up in value only to soon see his profit and even the entire premium value of the option disappear. By using the following rules for sound money management, this is less likely to occur:

1. When purchasing an option for a short-term move, sell half of your position if the price of the option doubles. This allows for both flexibility and protection. Many time markets will have a pullback or a consolidation. During these times, the price of the option you purchased, especially one that has a short time to expiration, will plunge rapidly (See Exhibit 4.3). By taking partial profits you not only protect yourself against this type of loss, but are also in a position to purchase additional options on a pullback without increasing your risk. During the two weeks prior to an options expiration, severe moves can produce unbelievable returns in short periods of time. For example, options on Treasury Bonds can be purchased for leverage of over 6,000 to 1, providing returns of 1,000% or more in less than two weeks. There have been cases where a low-priced option has risen over $1,000 during a single day and where bond options rose ten times in value within two weeks prior to expiration (See Exhibit 4.4).

   These examples are exciting—but, of course, it's not as easy as it looks. The three hardest parts of this trade are knowing when to use it, which option to use, and how to determine when to take profits and losses.

   First, let's look at when a short-term option trade should be initiated. When a trader buys an option in the last several

Exhibit 4.3
Purchasing an Option for Short-Term Move

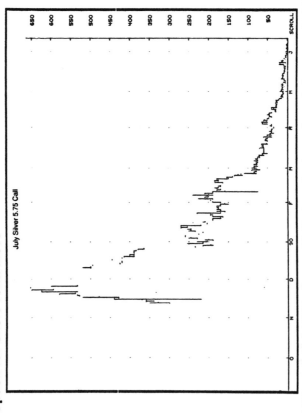

July Silver 5.75 Call

We watched this call (July 575 silver call) that we had purchased rise over $3,000 per option, only to plummet eventually to $0. (Fortunately, we followed our plan of taking profits on some of the position as the market rose and turning others into free trades to protect profits and capital.)

Exhibit 4.4
Severe Moves Increase Premiums

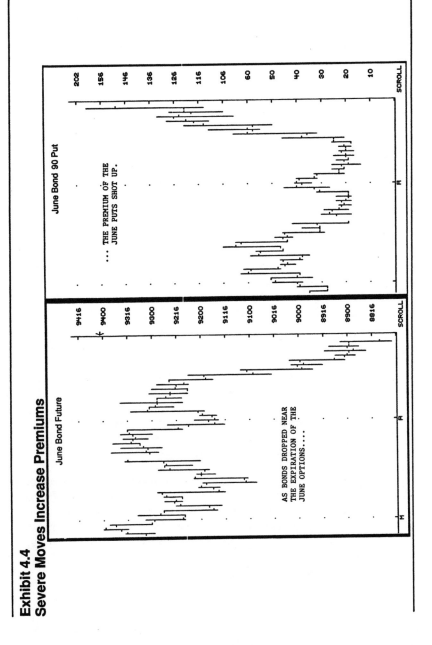

weeks of trading just because it is very low priced and provides substantial leverage, it is almost certain to lead to losses.
Your trading plan should allow you to only trade with the
trend of the market, and then to only initiate trades on a pull
back against that trend to obtain the most favorable entry point.
If this opportunity falls within the last two weeks of trading
and you feel an immediate move will occur, then you can initiate action to buy the appropriate option. Although purchasing
options two or three strike prices out-of-the-money cheaply
may seem attractive, unless the market makes a large move,
these options will not gain much in value.

The best option to purchase for short-term moves is the option
that is at-the-money or just out-of-the-money by one strike
price. These options have a higher probability of profit by
being more likely to gain in value if the market moves in your
favor.

Since purchasing short-term options is very speculative and
volatile, take profits on half of your position if the options double in value, thereby giving you a "free trade" for the balance
of the options. On the rest, there are no set rules, but let the
markets "tell you" when to take profits. Since option prices
quite often spike up during big rallies or declines, always be
on alert during these spikes to gain a favorable exit price.

2. There are two rules for taking profits with a longer term option
    purchase:

    a. If the option purchased goes into the money by more than
       two strike prices, take profits. This is both for money man-
       agement reasons, and because the option then becomes illiq-
       uid and difficult to trade. Additionally, at that point, usually
       so much premium is built up in the option, it is cheaper
       (from a margin standpoint) to take a futures position.

    b. Pick the strike price which corresponds with the resistance
       on the futures contract, and put an order in to sell an option
       at the same price for which you purchased your original op-
       tion (to turn the trade into a "Free Trade"). Doing this both
       increases your probability of profit and risk-reward ratio,
       and allows you to put on additional positions on a pullback.
       This will be discussed in detail in the next section.

SELECTING THE BEST OPTION TO PURCHASE BY ANALYZING YOUR VIEW OF THE MARKET

Some traders decide which option is the best one to purchase based on either the amount of money available in their trading account or their brokers recommendation. Obviously, neither of these are excellent methods for making this decision.

I recently had the occasion to do work on these principles when I decided to purchase silver call options. It was an easy decision to eliminate all but four options from consideration (the July silver 4.25 and 4.50 call, and the September silver 4.75 and 5.00 calls). This was because in-the-money options provided little leverage, further out-of-the-money options were too speculative, requiring the market to make an extremely large move before providing significant profits, and far from expiration option months were too illiquid to trade.

However, after several hours of analysis, I could find no reason to favor any of these four options over the other. They were all well priced, and provided excellent risk/reward. This prompted me to do a computer study of how these options would behave under various price and volatility changes in the future. The results were not only enlightening, but allowed me to fine tune my option selection process.

My first choice before doing computer analysis would have been September silver $5 call which could have been purchased for about 8 cents ($400). I based this on both the low premium cost and the fact that I felt that even if the market moved to my "stop out" point, I would be able to hold this option for several weeks at a loss of not more than 3 cents ($150) per option.

What was distressing to me was that if the market moved up 30 cents during this time period (a move of 8% of the contract value) this option would only gain about 5 cents ($250), really not much of a reward for a fairly significant move in a short time period.

On the opposite end of the spectrum was the July silver 4.25 call. This option would initially cost about $600 (50% more than the September $5 call). However, if the market moved to my stop point, this option would lose almost 4 times as much as the September $5 call, losing 2/3 of its value or $400, in a three week period. On the bright side, this option would gain 15 cents ($750) on a 30 cent move up. In comparing these four options the general principles I found were the following:

1. Closer to expiration options will appreciate faster if the market moves in your favor; however, because of their time decay, they will lose much faster if the market remains stable or moves against you;

2. Deferred month options will hold their value well in adverse conditions, but will not appreciate as rapidly (unless a major move occurs);

3. Close-to-the-money options cost more; however, they have a better chance to profit in normal market moves;

4. Further from-the-money options provide greater leverage, but require a larger move to profit.

What this all means, is that you must not only analyze market direction, but also have a general idea on market timing and velocity of the move. If you feel the market is likely to make a major move within a short time period, the best option to purchase would be close to expiration options. Conversely, if you feel the market is going to make a slow move up over a long period of time, select deferred month options. In major market moves, larger quantities of out-of-the-money options are a better choice; while in most normal moves, closer-to-the-money options should be selected.

THE FREE TRADE

The "Free Trade" is an option position that, when completed, is more commonly known as a vertical spread (bull or bear spread) (Exhibits 4.5, 4.7). In a vertical spread, both options are bought and sold at the same time. In the "Free Trade," first an option is purchased, and then at a later time, the out-of-the-money option is sold. This change makes a major difference in the risk-reward ratio for this position.

I do not usually recommend vertical spreads since I require that any trade initiated have a 10-1 risk-reward ratio and/or a 75% probability of profit. Most vertical spreads have no better than a 50% probability of profit and a 3-1 risk-reward (unless you sell an option that is almost worthless - which defeats your purpose of doing this position).

For example, being bullish the bonds, in May 1990, I purchased the September 94 call at 42 points ($656). I assigned a risk level of $300 to this position. (I would close it out if the option declined to 23 points or $359). My objective was to sell a September bond 100 call on a rally, also at 42 points for a profit objective of $6,000. This would provide a risk-reward ratio of 300/6,000 or 20-1.

If I had considered a bull spread instead at that time, I could have purchased the 94 call and sold the 96 call for about 32 points ($500). This would have given me a risk-reward of only 500/2,000 or 4-1.

Another benefit of the "Free Trade" is that after it is completed there is no margin, or capital necessary, or potential loss. This accomplishes several objectives.

First, it keeps your account intact if the market turns against you. For example, I completed free trades in corn and soybeans in April and May 1990, as the grain markets heated up. However, as quickly as they rose, they began to fall. Even though most of my original call purchases were at a loss, "Free Trade" positions provided protection from loss, because the option I sold was losing more!

Exhibit 4.5
Free Trade

STRATEGY:	Option Buying.
POSITION:	Bullish—Buy call —Later, on rally, sell higher call.
	Bearish—Buy put —Later, on decline, sell lower put.
MARKET TREND:	Strongly Bullish or Bearish.
MAXIMUM PROFIT:	Difference between strike price of option purchased and option sold.
POTENTIAL LOSS:	Limited to premium paid for option.
WHEN TO INITIATE:	When strong, immediate market move is expected and option premiums are low.
WHICH STRIKE PRICE AND EXPIRATION TO USE:	For shorter-term move, within 30 days for expiration of option series; if immediate move expected, use closest to expiration option and strike price closest to, or in-the-money.
	For long-term move, use option expiration with at least 60 days before expiration, and no more than three strike prices out-of-the-money.

Exhibit 4.6
Examples of Chart Pattern to Look for in Underlying Future

©1991 CQG, Inc. TQ 20/20

Option buying recommended as markets are likely to make big move in either direction.

Second, "The Free Trade" gives you time to unemotionally examine your position, without the panic other traders may be in as their profitable positions begin to nose-dive. With the protection of the "Free Trade," you can wait for emotions to subside and the market to give you a better indication of its next move. You can then decide whether you want to hold your position for your full profit potential (knowing you are completely protected from loss), or cash out and take your existing profits (Exhibits 4.7, 4.8).

The third benefit is that when these "Free Trades" are completed, since your original capital is protected, you can turn your attention elsewhere. You may find opportunities in other markets or even take advantage of a pullback in the market in which you have completed "Free Trades" to add more positions. This can now be accomplished without increasing original risk—since your first "Free Trades" are now risk-free!

It is difficult to closely monitor more than two or three net positions, especially in volatile markets. The "Free Trade" allows you to concentrate more fully on other situations and meet your objective of getting a "trading edge" over the markets by using options.

After the free trade is completed, there are three possible alternatives:

1. Hold your position until expiration, and exercise your long option if it is in the money;
2. If the market has moved against you, allow both options to expire worthless; or
3. You may decide at anytime to close out your position and take profits.

Your decision of which position to choose must be determined through your own trading plan and current view of the market.

The only "complaint" that I have heard about "The Free Trade" is that you are limiting your potential gain by hedging with the sale of the out-of-the-money call. Your profit is limited, however this detriment is more than offset by the "no loss" aspect of this trade. And, you can continue to add on to this position in the further out months on the next pullback. In effect, you can keep building this position without increasing your initial risk. This can allow for as much or even more profit than just holding your original position.

Exhibit 4.7
July Corn 270 Call

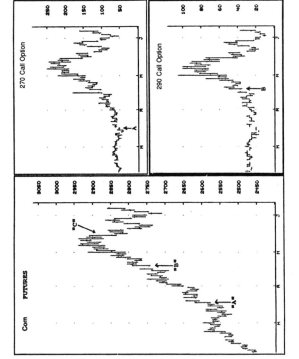

On March 14 at "A," we purchased the July corn 270 call at 4-1/2. After the market rallied to "B" on April 19, we sold the July corn 290 call at 4-3/4 to complete the free trade, because we were able to hold the position through the break in the market at "C." Also of importance is that the 270 call gained in value 20 cents during the April rally, and 10 cents in June, while the 290 call gained only 8 cents and 2 cents.

Exhibit 4.8
June Bond 90 Put

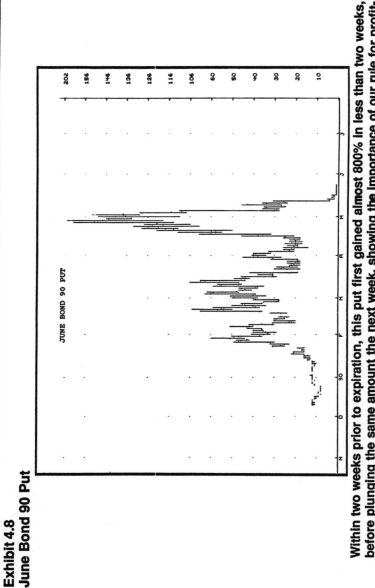

Within two weeks prior to expiration, this put first gained almost 800% in less than two weeks, before plunging the same amount the next week, showing the importance of our rule for profit-taking.

SYNTHETIC FUTURES POSITION

By using a combination of puts and calls, you can create a synthetic position with a profit potential that will closely approximate a futures contract or stock purchase with many benefits over just a net futures or options position. A bullish synthetic position is created by purchase of a call and the sale of a put, and a bearish synthetic is just the opposite. This position can be created to reflect both your views on the market and the amount of money you care to risk on the trade. When a credit is received from initiating this spread, in addition to this credit and potentially unlimited profit if the market moves in your favor, one can profit if the market remains neutral, and in some cases, even if the market moves against you!

Exhibit 4.9
Synthetic Futures Position

STRATEGY:	Synthetic Futures Position.
POSITION:	Bullish—Buy call, sell put.
	Bearish—Buy put, sell call.
MARKET TREND:	Potential of change of trend (previous trend broken); or upon reaction (pullback) in already trending market.
MAXIMUM PROFIT:	Unlimited.
POTENTIAL LOSS:	Theoretically unlimited.
	(Place $500 stop loss instructions with broker.)
WHEN TO INITIATE:	Market basing (topping) and unlikely to go substantially lower (higher).
WHICH STRIKE PRICE AND EXPIRATION TO USE:	Options that have 60 days or more before expiration. Buy option nearest-the-money. Sell option below last low (bullish) or above last high (bearish).
COMMENT:	Excellent position to take advantage of market trend, as short option pays for cost of long position; if initiated at credit, profit will be made even if it moves slightly against you.

For example, in the beginning of October 1985, I recommended a synthetic bullish position in the December S&P of purchasing the 195 call and selling the 175 put (Exhibit 4.10). I used these options because my trading plan called for closing out this position if the S&P closed below the 180 level (area of heavy support), and this position would have the least risk if that happened. (In any strategy containing an option sale, risk limits must be set to prevent potentially unlimited losses.) At that point, the loss in this position would be about $250. Additionally, I decided to use the 195 call and the 175 put because the combination of this position would give me a credit of $300, that would be our profit even if the market maintained its current trading range.

This position had a 75% probability of profit because I would profit in three out of four situations: 1) if the market moved higher; 2) if it remained neutral; or 3) if it moved slowly lower. Only if the market dropped suddenly would this position lose money.

This spread is a flexible strategy that can be changed to meet your views of the market. It is an excellent position when a futures contract is at heavy support or resistance levels.

Follow-up action should be taken on this strategy:

1. If the market moves against you, this position should be closed out prior to your short option being in the money (to prevent unlimited loss) or at a set loss level not exceeding $500; and

2. If the market moves in your favor, profits should be taken on the short put, and the long option turned into a "Free Trade" pursuant to the guidelines in the last section.

NEUTRAL OPTION POSITIONS

Selling options is a strategy that most public traders have stayed away from, both for a lack of understanding and a fear of potential loss (unlimited) that can occur. The professional trader, on the other hand, employs the option sale quite frequently (Exhibits 4.11, 4.12.).

Statistical research in this area is very interesting. Over 90% of the public when speculating in options purchase options; and the public loses in option trading over 90% of the time. Conversely, professional traders, who are the biggest sellers of option premium, profit a majority of the time.

The mathematical odds strongly favor the option seller. An option is a wasting asset (Exhibit 4.14). This is because an option is comprised

Exhibit 4.10
Examples of Chart Pattern to Look for in Underlying Future

©1991 CQG, Inc. TQ 20/20

Bullish synthetic futures position initiated of long 7 call, short 6 put at credit, as market has potentially triple bottomed and broken out of downtrend.

©1991 CQG, Inc. TQ 20/20

Synthetic futures position (long call, short put) initiated at credit as market analysis shows 75%+ probability of trading range or higher prices.

Exhibit 4.11
Option Sale

STRATEGY:	Neutral Option Spread.
POSITION:	Sell out-of-money put and call.
MARKET TREND:	Neutral.
MAXIMUM PROFIT:	Credit received when initiating position.
POTENTIAL LOSS:	Unlimited, if either strike price is exceeded. (Place stop loss order with broker.)
WHEN TO INITIATE:	Trading range markets with high volatility.
WHICH STRIKE PRICE AND EXPIRATION TO USE:	Use closest to expiration option and strike prices at least two futures moves out-of-the-money.
COMMENT:	Best initiated 15-45 days prior to expiration (period of maximum decay). Close out if underlying market approaches either strike price or 70% of premium collected.

---

of time value premium. The longer an option has until expiration, the more value it should have. However, each day the option will lose some of its time value. Therefore, if one buys an option, even if his assessment of the market is correct, each day the time value of his option will be decreasing. In fact, as discussed in Chapter 1, the time decay of out-of-the-money options is so great, that sometimes even a large move in favor of the option buyer will not produce a profit.

The neutral option strategy is initiated by the sale of an out-of-the-money put and call of the same month of an option. Since both options are out-of-the-money, and both contain only time value premium, each day time value is lost by both options. There are four significant factors in a trading plan for Neutral Option Positions:

1 The probable range of the future contract underlying the option prior to the expiration of the option.

2. Comparison of the relative volatility level of the option.

3. Calculation of the options that have the most disparity (overvaluation), which will determine which combinations of op-

Exhibit 4.12
Neutral Option Positions

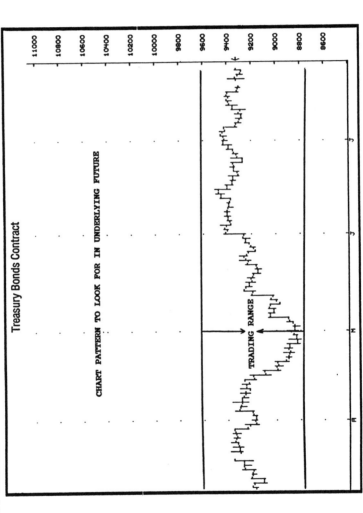

Treasury Bonds Contract

CHART PATTERN TO LOOK FOR IN UNDERLYING FUTURE

TRADING RANGE

Exhibit 4.13
Neutral Option Position in June Bonds (Short 86 Put and 96 Call)

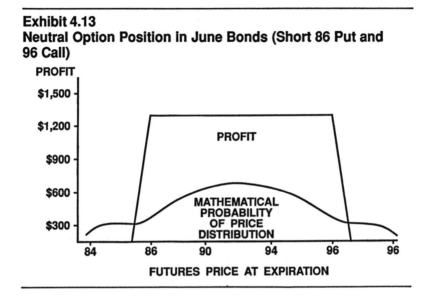

FUTURES PRICE AT EXPIRATION

tions have the highest probability of profit (and least likelihood of loss), and the most favorable risk to reward ratio; and

4. Principles of money management.

The first element of a strategy is determination of the probable range of the futures contract. Also considered at this point is the long and short term trend of the market and contract support and resistance.

The second factor is the relative volatility levels of the option. This is to determine whether the option contract has relatively high or low volatility (premium value). When high volatility occurs over an extended period of time, it is mathematically probable that the market will enter a trading range or consolidation period. It is, in fact, during severely trending markets that we experience the greatest discrepancies in option premium, as the option premium of out-of-money options can rise far in excess of their fair valuation, providing some of the best opportunities. Conversely, research has shown that in times of very low volatility, the market is likely to make a large move. Therefore, during these periods you should not initiate neutral option positions.

Computer generated charts are then used to calculate the most overvalued options. "Trade sheets" are prepared that provide not only the fair option value for all of the option months and strike prices, but what each option or combination of options will do, if the market moves in any direction at anytime in the future (Exhibits 4.14, 4.15, 4.16, 4.17).

Finally, proper money management methods are essential. Since you are not attempting to be predictive of market price or direction, management techniques are necessary for these strategies to be successful. These principles of money management include having enough margin available to maintain your "delta neutrality," to adjust a position up or down when the market moves strongly in either direction, and to trade only at times when the most significant opportunities are present.

You should sell options during the 60 days prior to an options' expiration (particularly during the last 30 days), since the time value decay of an option accelerates quite rapidly then. Choose strike prices that are beyond the expected range of the contract, above substantial resistance, and below strong support levels.

In addition to determining the expected range and resistance, you should also look at the risk-reward in selling an option. For example, if an option can be sold that is $2,000 more out-of-the-money with only $100 less premium received, your risk-reward in this trade is increased by 20 to 1 by choosing the further out-of-the-money option.

A final rule that you should follow is that unless an option has less than 30 days to expiration you should receive at least $250 in premium to make the option sale worthwhile. This is because with commission costs and slippage, you must receive a sufficient amount to make the sale worthwhile.

These positions should be closed out if:

1. The underlying future moves so that either option is within one strike price of being at-the-money;

2. The loss on the position exceeds $500; or

3. 75% of the potential option premium is collected.

Exhibit 4.14
Future Expected Value of September 74 Treasury Bonds Put at Different Futures Prices as It Approaches Expiration

VOLATILITY = 12.475%
INTEREST RATE = 8.5%
EXERCISE PRICE = 74

++++++++++++++++++++++++++PUTS+++++++++++++++++++++++++						
DAYS LEFT:	19	16	13	10	7	4	1
72'09	1'62	1'59	1'56	1'52	1'49	1'47	1'46
DEL	-.78	-.80	-.83	-.86	-.90	-.96	-1.00
72'13	1'56	1'52	1'49	1'46	1'42	1'39	1'38
DEL	-.76	-.79	-.81	-.84	-.89	-.95	-1.00
72'17	1'49	1'46	1'43	1'39	1'35	1'32	1'30
DEL	-.75	-.77	-.79	-.82	-.87	-.93	-1.00
72'21	1'44	1'40	1'36	1'32	1'28	1'24	1'22
DEL	-.73	-.75	-.77	-.80	-.85	-.91	-1.00
72'25	1'38	1'34	1'30	1'26	1'22	1'17	1'14
DEL	-.71	-.73	-.75	-.78	-.82	-.89	-.99
72'29	1'32	1'28	1'24	1'20	1'15	1'10	1'06
DEL	-.69	-.70	-.73	-.75	-.80	-.86	-.99
73'01	1'27	1'23	1'19	1'14	1'09	1'03	'62
DEL	-.67	-.68	-.70	-.73	-.77	-.84	-.98
73'05	1'22	1'18	1'13	1'08	1'03	'61	'55
DEL	-.64	-.66	-.68	-.70	-.74	-.80	-.96
73'09	1'17	1'12	1'08	1'03	'61	'55	'47
DEL	-.62	-.63	-.65	-.67	-.71	-.76	-.93
73'13	1'12	1'07	1'03	'62	'56	'49	'40
DEL	-.60	-.61	-.62	-.64	-.67	-.72	-.88

++++++++++++++++++++++++++PUTS+++++++++++++++++++++++++						
DAYS LEFT:	19	16	13	10	7	4	1
73'17	1'07	1'03	'62	'57	'50	'43	'33
DEL	-.58	-.59	-.60	-.61	-.64	-.68	-.83
73'21	1'02	'62	'57	'52	'45	'38	'27
DEL	-.56	-.56	-.57	-.58	-.60	-.63	-.76
73'25	'62	'58	'53	'47	'41	'33	'21
DEL	-.53	-.54	-.54	-.55	-.56	-.58	-.67
73'29	'58	'53	'48	'43	'36	'28	'16
DEL	-.51	-.51	-.51	-.52	-.52	-.53	-.57
74'01	'54	'49	'44	'39	'32	'24	'12
DEL	-.49	-.49	-.49	-.49	-.49	-.48	-.47
74'05	'50	'46	'41	'35	'29	'21	'08
DEL	-.46	-.46	-.46	-.46	-.45	-.43	-.37
74'09	'46	'42	'37	'32	'25	'17	'06
DEL	-.44	-.44	-.43	-.42	-.41	-.39	-.28
74'13	'43	'39	'34	'28	'22	'14	'04
DEL	-.42	-.41	-.40	-.39	-.37	-.34	-.21
74'17	'40	'35	'31	'25	'19	'12	'02
DEL	-.40	-.39	-.38	-.36	-.34	-.29	-.14
74'21	'37	'32	'28	'23	'17	'10	'01
DEL	-.37	-.36	-.35	-.33	-.31	-.25	-.09

Exhibit 4.15
Daily Trade Sheet for June Treasury Bonds

Volatility= 11.9%	Interest Rate= 8.5%								Days Out= 264	8-26-85					
+++++++++++++++CALLS+++++++++++++									++++++++++++++PUTS++++++++						
	68	70	72	74	76	78	80	82	68	70	72	74	76	78	80
68'00	2'34	1'47	1'30	'47	'28	'17	'09	'05	2'40	3'45	4'63	6'28	8'01	9'45	11'29
DEL	.49	.36	.28	.20	.13	.09	.06	.03	-.45	-.56	-.65	-.73	-.80	-.85	-.88
DIV	'14	'13	'12	'10	'08	'06	'04	'03	'14	'14	'12	'10	'08	'06	'04
69'00	3'03	2'10	1'29	'61	'38	'23	'13	'06	2'13	3'11	4'23	5'46	7'15	8'56	10'38
DEL	.54	.43	.33	.24	.17	.11	.07	.04	-.40	-.50	-.60	-.69	-.76	-.82	-.86
DIV	'14	'14	'13	'11	'09	'07	'05	'03	'14	'14	'13	'12	'09	'07	'05
70'00	3'40	2'39	1'52	1'14	'50	'31	'19	'11	1'53	2'45	3'50	5'03	6'31	8'04	9'47
DEL	.60	.49	.36	.29	.21	.14	.09	.06	-.35	-.45	-.55	-.65	-.73	-.79	-.84
DIV	'13	'14	'14	'13	'11	'08	'06	'04	'14	'14	'13	'11	'09	'07	
71'00	4'16	3'08	2'14	1'34	1'00	'41	25	'15	1'32	2'18	3'16	4'28	5'50	7'18	8'58
DEL	.64	54	.44	.34	.25	.17	.12	.08	-.30	-.40	-.50	-.60	-.69	-.76	-.81
DIV	'13	'14	'14	'14	'12	'10	'07	'05	'13	'14	'14	'14	'12	'10	'08
72'00	4'58	3'44	2'44	1'57	1'18	'53	'34	'21	1'14	1'58	2'50	3'55	5'08	6'35	8'07
DEL	.69	.59	.49	.39	.29	.21	.15	.10	-.26	-.35	-.45	-.55	-.64	-.72	-.78
DIV	'12	'14	'15	'14	'13	'11	'09	'07	'12	'14	'15	'14	'13	'11	'09
73'00	5'40	4'20	3'13	2'19	1'38	1'04	'44	'26	'63	1'37	2'23	3'21	4'32	5'54	7'22
DEL	.73	.64	.54	.44	.34	.25	.18	.12	-.22	-.30	-.40	-.50	-.60	-.68	-.75
DIV	'11	'13	'15	'15	'14	'12	'10	'08	'11	'13	'15	'15	'14	'13	'10
74'00	-6'24	4'62	3'49	2'49	-1'61	1'22	-'57	-'37	'51	1'19	1'62	2'55	3'60	5'12	6'39
DEL	.77	.69	.59	.49	.39	.30	.22	.15	-.18	-.26	-.35	-.45	-.55	-.64	-.71
DIV	'10	'13	'14	'15	'15	'13	'12	'09	'10	'14	'15	'15	'14	'13	'13
75'00	7'10	5'44	4'24	3'18	2'24	1'42	1'08	'47	'40	1'03	1'41	2'27	3'26	4'37	5'58
DEL	.80	.73	.64	.54	.44	.34	.26	.19	-.15	-.22	-.31	-.40	-.50	-.59	-.67
DIV	'09	'12	'14	'15	'15	'14	'13	'11	'09	'12	'14	'15	'15	'14	'13
76'00	7'62	6'27	5'02	3'54	2'53	2'02	1'26	'60	'32	'54	1'23	2'03	2'60	4'00	5'16
DEL	.83	.76	.68	.59	.49	.39	.30	.22	-.12	-.19	-.27	-.36	-.45	-.56	-.63
DIV	'08	'11	'13	'15	'15	'14	'12		'08	'11	'13	'15	'15	'14	'13
77'00	8'52	7'13	5'47	4'29	3'22	2'28	1'47	1'12	'25	'43	1'07	1'46	2'32	3'31	4'41
DEL	.85	.79	.72	.63	.54	.44	.35	.26	-.10	-.15	-.23	-.31	-.40	-.50	-.59
DIV	'07	'09	'12	'14	'15	'16	'15	'13	'07	'10	'12	'14	'15	'16	'15
++++++++++++++CALLS+++++++++++++									+++++++++++++++PUTS++++++++						
	68	70	72	74	76	78	80	82	68	70	72	74	76	78	80
78'00	9'43	8'00	6'30	5'07	3'58	2'58	2'06	1'30	'19	'34	'58	1'27	2'08	3'00	4'05
DEL	.87	.82	.76	.68	.58	.49	.39	.31	-.08	-.13	-.19	-.27	-.36	-.45	-.54
DIV	'06	'08	'11	'13	'15	'16	'16	'14	'06	'09	'11	'14	'15	'16	'16
79'00	10'35	8'54	7'16	5'51	4'33	3'27	2'33	1'51	'15	'27	'47	1'11	1'50	2'37	3'36
DEL	.88	.84	.79	.71	.63	.54	.44	.35	-.06	-.10	-.16	-.23	-.31	-.40	-.50
DIV	'05	'07	'10	'13	'15	'16	'16	'14	'05	'08	'10	'13	'15	'16	'16
80'00	11'28	9'44	8'03	6'34	5'11	3'63	2'63	2'11	'11	'21	'37	'62	'132	'213	'305
DEL	.90	.86	.81	.75	.67	.58	.49	.40	-.05	-.08	-.13	-.20	-.27	-.36	-.45
DIV	'04	'06	'09	'12	'14	'16	'16	'16	'04	'07	'09	'12	'14	'16	'16

Daily trade sheet for June Treasury Bonds giving theoretical option values at different futures prices.
"DEL" is the percentage the option value will change as compared to the futures.
"DIV" is the amount the option value should change if volatility increases or decreases by 1%
(Com-Tech Software)

Exhibit 4.16

Option:	US	Valuation Date: 5/19/91	Interest: 8.75	Div/For: 0.00

Theoretical Profit and Loss

Futures	Time: 5/19/91	7/06/91	8/24/91
9000	-208	-147	-128
9020	-146	-117	-52
9108	-122	-53	-12
9128	-100	-28	28
9216	-46	-6	104
9304	-30	12	124
9324	-18	27	124
9412	-8	38	124
9500	-2	45	124
9520	0	48	124
9608	-1	48	124
9628	-5	43	124
9716	-13	34	124
9804	-24	22	124
9824	-38	5	124
9912	-55	-15	52
10000	-112	-38	12

Futures Prices

Sim	U	MY	Spread	Value
*	Y	M1		9518
	Y	U1	-26	9424
	Y	Z1	-23	9401
	Y	H2	-20	9313
	Y	M2	-17	9228
	Y	U2	-16	9212
	Y	Z2	-15	9129
	Y	H3		

Range: FUTURES
From: 9000
To: 10000

Contour: TIME
- - - : 5/19/91
- - : 7/06/91
—— : 8/24/91

Exhibit 4.17

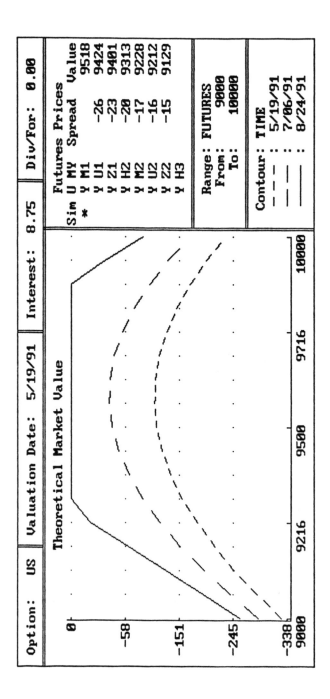

| Option: | US | Valuation Date: | 5/19/91 | Interest: | 8.75 | Div/For: | 0.00 |

Theoretical Market Value

Futures Prices

Sim	U	MY	Spread	Value
*	Y	M1		9518
	Y	U1	-26	9424
	Y	Z1	-23	9401
	Y	H2	-20	9313
	Y	M2	-17	9228
	Y	U2	-16	9212
	Y	Z2	-15	9129
	Y	H3		

Range: FUTURES
From: 9000
To: 10000

Contour: TIME
— — : 5/19/91
— — : 7/06/91
——— : 8/24/91

RATIO OPTION SPREAD

This position consists of buying an option that is close-to-the-money and selling two options further out-of-the-money (Exhibits 4.18, 4.19). It works particularly well in volatile markets, especially those that are bullishly oriented. The reason for this is that the options that are the far out-of-the-money options become over priced because of the demand for "cheap" options in these types of markets.

An example of a ratio spread would be purchasing an April gold 440 call and selling (2) April gold 500 calls at a $300 credit. (This is the way you give the order to your broker.) The floor broker, for example, will purchase the 440 call for $2,400, while simultaneously selling (2)

Exhibit 4.18
Ratio Option Spread

STRATEGY:	Ratio Option Spread.
POSITION:	Bullish—Buy call, sell 2 or more out-of-money calls.
	Bearish—Buy put, sell 2 or more out-of-money puts.
MARKET TREND:	Neutral/slightly trending.
MAXIMUM PROFIT:	Difference between strike prices of long and short options.
POTENTIAL LOSS:	Unlimited if underlying futures contract exceeds strike price of options sold.
WHEN TO INITIATE:	Option premiums high; market has made large move and is likely to continue to trend.
WHICH STRIKE PRICE AND EXPIRATION TO USE:	Buy strike price at least a limit move out-of-the-money; sell options at least 2 strike prices away. Use option expiration at least 3 months from strategy initiation.
COMMENT:	Excellent position to initiate after market has made a large move and option premiums are high, especially if credit is received, as spread will be profitable if market moves against you, remains neutral, or reacts as expected.

Exhibit 4.19
Examples of Chart Pattern to Look for in Underlying Future

©1991 CQG, Inc. TQ 20/20

Treasury bonds had made a near vertical move of eight points in one month, causing out-of-the-money calls to expand greatly in premium valuation. The ratio spread of long 76 call and short 80 and 82 call, even though initiated at a small debit, had an excellent probability of profit.

©1991 CQG, Inc. TQ 20/20

The Swiss Franc moved up 1,000 points from May through October, and option premiums were very high. The ratio spreads of long the 46 call and short two 49 calls was initiated at a $200 credit. This spread has a very high probability of profit, and had a profit range from 0 through 5,200.

500 calls at $1,350 each. You, therefore, pay out $2,400 but receive back $2,700, for a net of $300 credit. This $300 credit is very important in preventing losses if your prediction of market direction is wrong.

This trade would be profitable if gold moves down $440 or up over $110, for a range of profitability of over $550 (Exhibit 4.20). If April gold expires at any dollar value from $440 to $0, both the calls purchased and the calls sold are worthless. Therefore, you lose the $2,400 paid for the 440 call, however, make $2,700 you received for the (2) 500 calls, for a net profit of $300.

However, if the gold contract expires in the range between $440 and $500 (which is what you would be predicting in doing this spread) you are much more profitable. In that case, you still collect the $2,700 premium for selling the 500 calls as they are expiring worthless; you still lose the $2,400 premium paid for the 440 calls; however, you make $100 for every $1 gold closes above $440. The chart below also shows the amount of money that you will make in addition to the $300 credit at each price level, which ranges from $300 at the 440 level to $6,300 at the $500 level (Exhibit 4.21).

Now before everyone rushes out to put on this spread, let's look at the area where potential problems arise. (Remember, there is no "sure thing" in trading: if it looks too good to be true, it is!) There are only trades that are profitable over large ranges or have high probabilities of profits. Ironically, the problem in this trade arises if the market does even better than predicted. The chart also shows what happens to profits over the 500 level, until finally at $560 per ounce you begin to loose money! In effect, you lose $100 for each $1 gold closes over $560 per ounce.

Because of this, strict risk management requires closing out the position if the price of the contract rises above the strike price of the calls sold. In this case, it would require closing the position if gold closed over $500 per ounce. If this were to occur quickly, say in one month after initiating, this would cause a loss. (However, if you were able to hold the spread for three weeks or more, the decay of the premium for the short options should act to prevent any loss in this position even if you were forced to close it out.)

Why does this spread work so well? Because the two options sold contain only "time value" which constantly decays each day as the option approaches maturity. In this example, the two 500 calls you sold will decay in value much quicker than the 440 call since the 500 calls are much further out-of-the-money.

Exhibit 4.20
Range of Profit

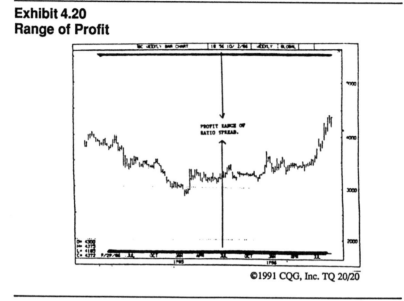

©1991 CQG, Inc. TQ 20/20

Exhibit 4.21
Profit/Loss of Gold Ratio Spread

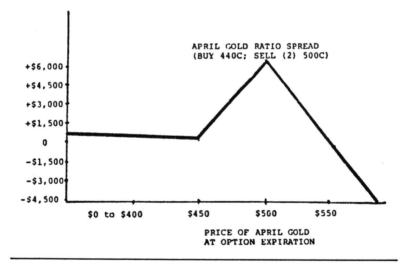

The chart formation we are interested in is always the same—a market making an almost straight up vertical move. This type of bullish formation is necessary since you are seeking to sell multiples of the furthest out-of-the-money options at the highest possible premium. This is the real *secret* of the best ratio spread—being able to obtain extraordinarily high premiums for the out-of-the-money calls that you sell, and this type of bullish market provides your best premiums.

For example, last year, with March copper trading at 115 (after moving almost straight up from 60) you could buy one March copper 120 call and sell two March copper 140 calls and receive a 100 point or $250 credit. The 140 calls at that time were the furthest out-of-the-money calls available, and could be sold at 700 points each. Being able to receive a large amount of premium not only provides more cash for your account, but also allows significant protection if the market consolidates or turns around and heads lower (Exhibit 4.22).

In the March copper ratio spread, the type of action you were looking for was a slow upward movement in the market with March copper expiring at the 140 level. This would provide you with a 20 cent ($5,000) profit on your long call; no loss on your short calls as they would expire worthless; and you would also collect your initial $250 credit.

The only problem area is when March copper begins to exceed the 140 level. Since you would be short two options and only long one, you begin to lose 2 cents on the options that you are short and gain only 1 cent on the long option for a loss of 1 cent ($250) for every penny copper moves over $1.40.

It is for this reason that it is best to place mandatory stops on all ratio spreads at the level of your short calls. That is, if March copper were to exceed $1.40 at any time, you should close out the position. The amount of profit or loss on this spread at that point would depend on the time when copper reached this level. As seen in Exhibit 4.23, if copper did not reach this level until December 1, you would have a profit on this spread.

The reason for the amount of time for copper to exceed this level is important. The overvalued out-of-the-money calls will begin to quickly lose their value because of the time decay of these options as the contract approaches expiration. However, the opposite will happen to the long 120 call if the market makes a slow move up. This call would be "in-the-money" and start to gain in value. In fact, during the last 60 days before expiration of the option, with copper trading between 125

Exhibit 4.22
Ratio Option Spread (Copper)

The only problem is when March copper begins to exceed the 140
level. Since we are short 2 options and only long 1, we begin to
lose 2 cents on the options that we are short and gain only 1 cent
on the long option for loss of 1 cent ($250) for every penny copper
moves over $1.40. The chart illustrates how profits begin to erode
to a point where at $1.60 we begin to experience losses.

Exhibit 4.23
Ratio Option Spread (Copper)

Futures Contr: CPNY	Valuation Date: 11/01/88	
Futures	Time:11/01/88	Theoretical Market Value 12/01/88	1/01/89
11500	92	67	24
11875	121	99	46
12250	152	138	82
12625	183	184	132
13000	212	233	199
13375	234	282	279
13750	247	327	368
14125	248	361	458
14500	234	381	540
14875	202	381	602
15250	149	358	636
15625	75	308	633
16000	-22	230	590
16375	-143	122	501
16750	-287	-15	368
17125	-453	-181	193
17500	-641	-375	-13

and 135, you could expect many days to see that the option purchased gains in value, while the out-of-the-money calls that had been sold lose value, thereby providing profit on both sides of the transaction.

The main benefit of this position is its flexibility in allowing you to profit without having to predict the exact direction of the market. It allows you to make maximum use of the overvaluation and disparity in price of the out-of-the-money options. Because of this, ratio spreads are one of our favorite option strategies.

REVERSE RATIO SPREAD

The reverse ratio spread is an excellent position to enter into in extremely volatile option markets such as coffee, orange juice, pork bellies or cotton, and even in the currencies or financial markets in turbulent times or before major reports or events (Exhibits 4.24, 4.25).

This spread is initiated by selling an at-the-money put and call, and purchasing two or more out-of-the-money puts and calls. You would like

---

Exhibit 4.24
Reverse Ratio Spread

STRATEGY:	Reverse Ratio Spread.
POSITION:	Sell at-the-money put and call. Buy two or more out-of-the-money puts and calls.
MARKET TREND:	Neutral—but likely to make large moves in either direction.
MAXIMUM PROFIT:	Unlimited.
POTENTIAL LOSS:	Difference between the strike prices of options bought and sold.
WHEN TO INITIATE:	Technical pattern of market suggests large move likely to occur, but direction is uncertain.
WHICH STRIKE PRICE AND EXPIRATION TO USE:	Options that have 60 days or more before expiration. Sell put and call options at-the-money; purchase 2 puts and 2 calls two strike prices out-of-the-money.
COMMENT:	When credit received, position will be profitable if market moves in either direction.

Exhibit 4.25
Reverse Ratio Spread (Treasury Bonds)

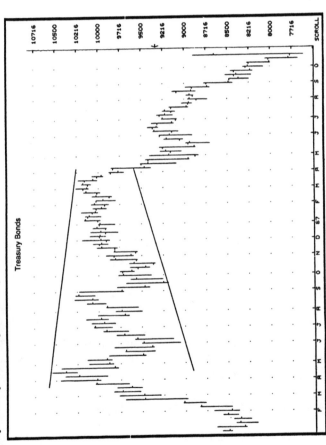

Bonds moved into a 1-year consolidation triangle suggesting a large move in either direction and option volatility had dropped to historically low levels.

Exhibit 4.26
Profit/Loss of Reverse Ratio Position

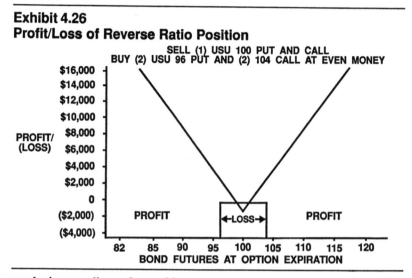

to obtain a credit on the position, or at worst a break-even on the debits versus credits.

As seen in the profit loss graph below, this position is profitable when the market makes a large move in either direction (Exhibit 4.26). It is similar to the Neutral Option Position in that it is unnecessary to determine the exact direction of the market, however in this case, you want to be able to deduce that a large move is about to occur. It is for this reason, this spread is particularly effective in the agricultural commodities during critical growing times, and the currencies during politically turbulent periods.

To give this trade time to mature, you should initiate the position using options having about six months to expiration. Since the maximum loss occurs at expiration if the underlying market fails to move substantially, you should close out this trade 30-45 days prior to expiration, if the expected move fails to occur.

IN-THE-MONEY OPTION DEBIT SPREAD

The "In-The-Money Option Debit Spread" is a position that can be used to take advantage of a trending market, and also provide significant benefits over a straight "long or short" future position (Exhibits 4.27, 4.28).

It is initiated by purchasing an in-the-money option containing intrinsic (real) value, and selling an out-of-the-money option containing

---

Exhibit 4.27
In-The-Money Option Debit Spread

STRATEGY:	In-The-Money Debit Spread.
POSITION:	Bullish—Buy in-the-money call, sell further out-of-the-money call. Bearish—Buy in-the-money put, sell further out-of-the-money put.
MARKET TREND:	Bullish or bearish.
MAXIMUM PROFIT:	Differences between strike prices of options.
POTENTIAL LOSS:	Limited to debit paid when position is initiated.
WHEN TO INITIATE:	Trending market with higher option premium (volatility) for out-of-the-money option.
WHICH STRIKE PRICE AND EXPIRATION TO USE:	Options that have 60 days or less before expiration. Buy option in or near the money. Sell most overvalued option.
COMMENT:	Excellent position to take advantage of market trend, disparity in option premium and time decay of the out-of-the-money option.

---

only time value. If the market moves in the intended direction, the in-the-money option will gain value much faster than its out-of-the-money option, which, in fact, sometimes will lose its value, even as the market moves in its favor! It can also provide substantial protection in a neutral market, as you will collect premium from the declining value of the out-of-the-money option that you have sold.

During Oct.-Dec., 1990 while the market was in a trading range between 315 and 330, although the market was neutral, an in-the-money debit spread of long the 315 call and short the 330 put would have been profitable and have collected the entire debit during this period. This is because while the 315 call contained "intrinsic" (real) value, the further out-of-the-money option (330 call) contained "time" value. The time value in the 330 call option decayed every day as the option moved closer to expiration (Exhibit 4.29).

Therefore, the 330 call lost much of its value on a continual basis, while the in-the-money option (the 315 call) lost little of its value since

Exhibit 4.28
Chart Patterns to Look for in Underlying Future (A Trending Market)

Exhibit 4.29
In-The-Money Debit Spreads (S&P 500)

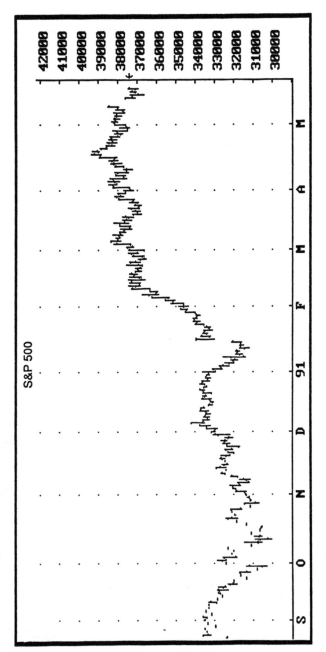

In-the-money debit spreads were recommended in late 1990 and early 1991 to take advantage of trending market and high premium for the out-of-the-money call options.

it contained very little time value to begin with. Because of these reasons, this type of position can be successful if the market moves in the direction that you predicted (put spread - lower; call spread - higher), or even if the market is stable! In addition to increasing your odds of success on a trade, this position also allows you to take advantage of disparity in option pricing (overvaluation), and the time decay of option premium.

In the past, traders have avoided using the in-the-money options, since they are expensive and provide very little leverage—which is one of the significant benefits of using options. They can also be relatively illiquid, causing slippage (losses arising from the difference between the bid and ask) when entering and exiting the trade. However, the benefits from using these in-the-money options can far outweigh the disadvantages because you can construct a position that takes advantage of:

1. The trend of the market.
2. The overvaluation of the out-of-the-money options.
3. The time decay of the out-of-the-money options.
4. The tendency of the in-the-money options to hold their value better than out-of-the-money options under most market circumstances.

The best conditions for using this position are:

1. A trending market.
2. Markets where the out-of-the-money options are trading at a premium of at least 20% over the in-the-money options.

Another advantage of this strategy is the need for much less capital to enter a position thereby allowing both more leverage and diversification of funds. While a bullish future's position in the S&P 500 requires more than $20,000 margin, our "debit spread" above requires only about a $2,500 premium, a reduction of almost 90%.

Finally, this position can also effectively be used as a hedge for your cash or future portfolio. For example, if you own a stock portfolio, put positions can be constructed to hedge your downside risk at a minimum cost. Similar hedges can also be constructed to protect bond, currency, metal, and agricultural positions.

CALENDAR SPREAD

The calendar spread is initiated by selling an option of close-in-maturity and purchasing the same option of a later expiration (Exhibits 4.30, 4.31).

The option sold will lose its time value at a much greater rate as it approaches maturity. As decay of option time value accelerates in the final 60 days prior to expiration, this is the best time to initiate the calendar spread. At that time, this strategy has a high probability of profit because of the severe decay in time value. The objective of this position is to profit from the more rapid time decay of the close to expiration option.

For example, on November 1, 1990, a calendar spread could have been constructed in crude oil options by purchasing the January 36 call and selling the December 36 call at a debit of 50. Both options were out-of-the-money (with December crude being at 3300 and January at 3200), and contained only time value. However, since the December op-

---

Exhibit 4.30
Calendar Spread

STRATEGY:	Calendar Spread.
POSITION:	Sell near-month call (put). Buy far-month call (put).
MARKET TREND:	Neutral or trending.
MAXIMUM PROFIT:	Unlimited after short options expires.
POTENTIAL LOSS:	Unlimited (theoretically), but short option loss should, in most cases, be covered by gain in long option value.
WHEN TO INITIATE:	60 days prior to option expiration to take advantage of decay in option premium of option sold.
WHICH STRIKE PRICE AND EXPIRATION TO USE:	Sell closest-to-expiration option series, buy next furthest out; use strike prices depending on market outlook.
COMMENT:	Excellent spread to take advantage of option premium time value decay while still having protection from adverse move.

Exhibit 4.31
Calendar Spread (Swiss Franc)

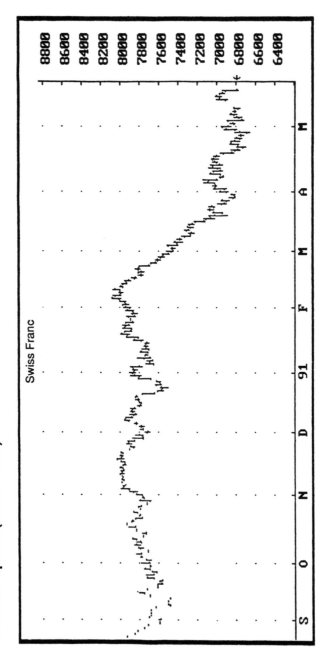

Swiss Franc

The calendar spread was recommended in March and April 1991 to take advantage of the high
option premium in the expiring May Swiss Franc option contract.

tion had only 14 days until expiration, it would decay much faster, whether the market went higher, lower, or remained stable. This position had the further benefit of the December option having higher volatility than the January options.

Closer to expiration options frequently have higher volatility than further out options. In 1991 this occurred quite often in many markets, including the currencies, bonds, and cattle. Anytime volatility is 20% or more higher in the front months, calendar spreads should be considered.

After the expiration of the short option, you should then have an objective of turning the long option into a "free trade," if the market moves in your favor, or just close out the remaining option if it doesn't.

OTHER COMMON OPTION STRATEGIES

The benefits and disadvantages of many option strategies are outlined in Exhibit 4.32. (Although it is impossible to discuss all of the many different positions that can be created by combining or mutating other option strategies, the most commonly used strategies are summarized here.)

I am not going to discuss these strategies in detail for several reasons. First, I see no reason to duplicate the many fine books in our bibliography that describe these positions adequately; and second, I wish to consider only strategies that can give you an advantage ("trading edge") by presenting you with favorable risk/reward ratios or a high probability of profit.

HEDGING WITH OPTIONS

Hedging strategies have been commonly employed by farmers, producers, distributors, and institutions to lock in costs, profits, or limit potential losses. Prior to the introduction of options in the 1980s, the futures market was commonly used for these purposes.

For example, a jewelry manufacturer who needs to purchase silver in the next six months, could purchase a six month silver futures contract at today's price to lock in his cost of silver. Similarly, a wheat farmer, with wheat trading at $3 per bushel and the cost of production at $2.25 per bushel, could sell his wheat on the futures market even though it would not be ready in the fields for several months, and lock in a profit of 75 cents per bushel. And, companies that deal with other foreign countries and must contract in advance would use currencies fu-

Exhibit 4.32

MOST COMMON OPTION STRATEGIES FOR ALL MARKETS			
OPTION SPREAD STRATEGY	**POSITION**	**CHARACTERISTICS**	**BEST TIME TO USE**
NEUTRAL STRATEGIES			
STRANGLE	Sell out-of-the-money put and call.	Maximum use of time value decay.	Trading range market with volatility peaking.
GUTS	Sell in-the-money put and call.	Receive large premium.	Options have time premium and market in trading range.
ARBITRAGE	Purchase and sale similar options simultaneously.	Profit certain if done at credit.	Any time credit received.
CONVERSION	Buy futures, buy at-the-money put and sell out-of-the-money call.	Profit certain if done at credit.	Any time credit received.
BOX	Sell calls and puts same strike prices.	Profit certain if done at credit.	Any time credit received.
BUTTERFLY	Buy at-the-money call (put) sell 2 out-of-the-money calls (puts) and buy out-of-the-money call (put).	Profit certain if done at credit.	Any time credit received.
CALENDAR	Sell near-month, buy far-month, same strike price.	Near-month time value decay faster.	Small debit, trading range market.
MIXED STRATEGIES			
RATIO CALL	Buy call, sell calls of higher strike price.	Neutral, slightly bullish.	Large credit and difference between strike price of option bought and sold.

Exhibit 4.32 (Continued)

MOST COMMON OPTION STRATEGIES FOR ALL MARKETS			
OPTION SPREAD STRATEGY	POSITION	CHARACTERIS-TICS	BEST TIME TO USE
STRADDLE PURCHASE	Buy put and call.	Options will lose time value premium quickly.	Options under-valued and market likely to make a big move.
COVERED CALL	Buy future—sell call.	Collect premium on calls sold.	Neutral—slightly bullish.
COVERED PUT	Sell future—sell put.	Collect premium of puts sold.	Neutral—slightly bearish.
SYNTHETIC FUTURES POSITION	Buy call (put). Sell put (call).	Neutral, slightly trend-ing market.	Receive credit, op-tion sold far-out-of-the-money.
BULLISH STRATEGIES			
BUY CALL	Most bullish option position.	Loss limited to pre-mium.	Undervalued option with volatility in-creasing.
SELL PUT	Neutral-bullish op-tion position.	Profit limited to debit.	Small debit, bullish market.
VERTICAL BULL-CALLS	Buy call, sell call of higher strike price.	Loss limited to debit.	Small debit, bullish market.
VERTICAL BULL-PUTS	Sell put, buy put of higher strike price.	Loss limited to price difference.	Large credit, bullish market.
BEARISH STRATEGIES			
BUY PUT	Most bearish option position.	Loss limited to pre-mium.	Undervalued option with volatility in-creasing.
SELL CALL	Neutral-bearish op-tion position.	Profit limited to pre-mium.	Option overvalued, market flat, bearish.
VERTICAL BEAR-PUTS	Buy at-the-money put, sell out-of-the-money put.	Loss limited to debit.	Small debit, bearish market.
VERTICAL BEAR-CALLS	Sell call, buy call of higher strike price.	Loss limited to strike price difference minus credit.	Large credit, bear-ish market.

tures to make certain that fluctuations in the currencies market would not adversely effect them.

However, the introduction of options in the 1980s brought more tools and flexibility for hedgers' needs. For example, the wheat farmer instead of selling his wheat at $3, and not being able to participate in any further price rise, could then use put options to protect his profits, and still be in a position to make more money if the wheat market went higher.

These strategies are not limited to farmers, producers and manufacturers. Any trader of a stock or commodity can also use options for hedging. Let's examine the three most popular methods of hedging:

1. Purchasing puts to protect a long position (or calls to protect the short position);
2. Selling calls to add income to an account; and
3. "No-Loss, Cost-Free" hedging.

1. PURCHASING A PUT FOR PROTECTION

The main benefit of purchasing a put to protect a long position is that it will provide absolute price protection if the market begins to decline. For example, assume that a trader has purchased a June S&P 500 contract at 335 and the market has now moved up to 365 and begins to consolidate. A trader with a long position and profits of $15,000 per contract could be very concerned as to whether a severe correction is about to take place. Although, a "stop" order could conceivably be used to protect his profits, many times a stop will not provide sufficient protection if events occur overnight or if the market begins dropping very rapidly. Further, it can be frustrating when the trader finds himself "stopped out" of a good position, which then begins to take off in his favor.

A better method here would be to purchase a S&P 355 put. By using less than 10% of the profits of the trade (about $1,000 in this case), a put can be purchased that will provide absolute price protection below the 355 level. This means that profits of $10,000 can be locked in, and unlimited profits are still available if the market continues to move higher (Exhibit 4.33).

Exhibit 4.33
Purchasing a Put for Protection (S&P 500—355 Put)

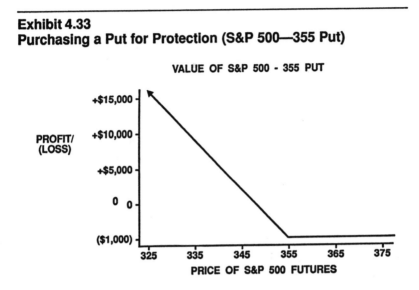

VALUE OF S&P 500 - 355 PUT

PROFIT/(LOSS)

PRICE OF S&P 500 FUTURES

As the price of the S&P 500 *declines*, the put becomes more valuable and offsets any loss in the futures contract.

As the price of the S&P 500 *increases*, the futures contract becomes more profitable.

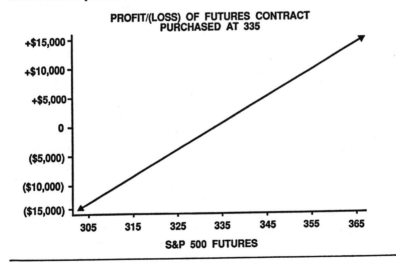

PROFIT/(LOSS) OF FUTURES CONTRACT
PURCHASED AT 335

S&P 500 FUTURES

2. SELLING CALLS FOR INCOME

Using the same example as above, the trader may decide that the market is again consolidating after moving from 335 to 365, and wish to add additional income to his account during this consolidation phase. To accomplish this, the trader would sell a 375 call and collect this premium for his account. The major benefit of this position over the purchase of put is that in a consolidating market, this strategy will add substantial income to your account on top of your profits, where the put will be a drain on your profits. However, the sale of calls provides no substantial protection against a large break in the market, unlike the put purchase.

3. "NO-LOSS COST-FREE" OPTION HEDGING

The best method of protecting positions is a combination of number 1 and 2 through a "No-Loss Cost-Free" hedging method. This allows you to use benefits of both strategies.

Quite often in the markets we are faced with tough decisions regarding giving up a "sure thing" for a potentially more valuable prize. For example, after the crude oil exploded, traders had profits of thousands of dollars per position. However, because of the world conditions, many were concerned about not only being able to hold onto as much of this profit as possible, but protecting their capital in case the market dropped as quickly as it had risen. They also were insecure with stop loss orders, feeling they provided little protection against a drop in the market, since the oil market is subject to extreme overnight moves, based on political conditions around the world. Further, because of the explosive nature of the market, traders were concerned if they placed a "stop" too close to the position, only to see the market continue on in their favor without them. On the other hand, placing a stop order far away from the market could subject them to much larger losses.

Fortunately, there was a much easier way to protect profits, while still allowing them to make additional profit if the market continued in their favor. And, all of this could be accomplished for no additional out-of-pocket expense! Imagine being offered a free insurance policy to cover all of your assets from any potential problems or disaster without costing you any additional money. This is what is have available to you by the proper use of options.

How do you accomplish this? In the case of the crude oil market, where you are long a futures contract (expecting the price to go higher) you first purchase a put option. Remember a put option becomes more valuable as the price goes lower.

Let's assume that you purchased a crude oil futures contract at $20, and after it rose to $40 you purchased the 35 put option for $1,000. If oil were to drop, this would provide absolute protection of any profits below your put's strike price of $35. Since you had purchased your futures contracts at under $20, you are in effect "locking in" most of your profits with no chance for loss no matter what happens.

Let's assume that overnight large previously undiscovered fields of oil are found and the price of crude drops more than one half to $15. This would cause your original contract that you had purchased at $20 to have a loss of 500 points x $10 a point or $5,000. However, your $35 put would now be worth $20,000 ($35 strike price minus $15 actual price or $2,000 x $10 a point or $20,000). Even this type of catastrophic event leaves you with a profit of $15,000. And, the best part is if oil continues higher, you will still be able to profit from the appreciation of the market.

The second factor of the protective option strategy, "no-loss, cost-free hedging," is to sell a call to pay for the put purchased. If you continue to just pay for the protection by way of the puts, it can eventually become pretty expensive if the market stays in a trading range. This is because the options expire in a definite amount of time, and if the market just remains in a trading range, as markets often do, you will have to continue purchasing new puts and paying substantial amounts in premium.

Therefore, to pay for the put you purchased, I recommend selling an "out-of-the-money" crude oil call option. In this case you could sell a $45 call, which would not only entirely pay for the purchase of the $35 put, but still allow you $5,000 of additional profit if the market continued moving in your favor. Profits are limited to $45, if the market continued past that level. However, since the market had already moved over 100% from its lows at the beginning of the year, and you were still allowing for another more than 10% rise in prices, this small risk of having future profits somewhat limited is well worth the financial and emotional protection this position provides.

"No-loss, cost-free hedging" therefore provides for a win-win trade no matter what happens. If the market goes down, your capital and a percentage of your profits are protected from loss.

Using the same example as in number 1, after the S&P 500 rises from 335 to 365, you institute the no-loss cost-free hedging by purchasing the 355 put and selling the 375 call. In this instance, you are able to purchase the put for 250 points and sell the call for 350. By doing this you have locked in your profits of $10,000, similar to number one above; however, instead of having to pay $1,500 for the option, you are in fact paid $500 which is yours to keep on top of your profits. This is through the sale of the 375 call. You are also still able to receive an additional $5,000 in profits from this position if the market continues to rally.

The only negative that can be said about this trade at all is that your profits are limited to the 375 level. However, since the market had already made a substantial move and you are still allowing for another 1000 point price rise, the small risk of having futures profits somewhat limited is well worth the financial and emotional protection this position provides. Further, if the market began to show substantial signs of breaking out from this consolidation, the position could be closed out, allowing for unlimited profits again.

With "No-loss, cost-free" hedging, if the market goes down, all of your capital and a good percentage of your profits is protected from loss. If the market moves sideways, you have neither gained nor lost from your strategy, since you received a credit when you initiated this position. And finally, if the market moved in your favor (although this insurance turned out to be unnecessary) at least you did not pay for it, you were not "stopped out" of your position as you could have been with a stop order and you were still able to make additional profits on your trades (and in all cases, you were able to sleep well at night knowing your capital and most of your profits were protected).

Exhibit 4.34 examines the results of these and other possible hedging strategies in different market scenarios.

Exhibit 4.34
Results of Using Hedge/Income Strategies on $360,000 Stock Portfolio

Standard & Poor's Futures with 30 Days to Expiration = 360; 350 Put = $850; 360 Put = $1,750; 360 Call = $1,750; 370 Call = $850

STRATEGY	STRATEGY CHARACTERISTICS	REQUIREMENT FOR PROFIT	ACTION	MARKET MOVEMENT	STRATEGY PROFIT/LOSS	STRATEGY GAIN/LOSS
Put Purchase	High cost/risk is loss of option premium; reward limited to prevention of loss of stock or bond portfolio value; requires good skill in timing and premium evaluation.	Loss of premium results unless significant down-side move occurs.	Buy 2 360 Puts	Flat Decline to 350 Increase to 370	-3,500 +3,000 -3,500	-14% 12% -14%
Call Sale	Reward limited to amount of premium; limits profit potential of underlying portfolio, requires good skill in timing and premium evaluation.	Will add income to portfolio in flat or bear market, but can limit profit of underlying positions in bull market.	Sell 2 370 Calls	Flat Decline to 350	+1,700 +1,700	+6.8% +6.8%
Sell Future	Unlimited risk/reward requires maximum skill in timing.	Can provide hedge against loss in declining market, but can limit profit of underlying positions in bull market.	Sell 20 Futures	Flat Decline to 350 Increase to 370	0 +5,000 -5,000	0 +20% -20%
Neutral Option	Reward equal to amount of premium collected. Does not require prediction of market direction; requires good market monitoring and premium evaluation skill.	Underlying future remains in trading range of puts and calls sold; however, can be "rolled up or down".	Sell 2 350 Puts and Sell 2 370 Calls	Flat Decline to 350 Increase to 370	+3,400 +3,400 +3,400	+13.6% +13.6% +13.6%
Buy Put Sell Call ("No-Loss Cost Free")	Eliminates downside risk without premium cost; does not require prediction of market direction or monitoring.	Excellent strategy for portfolio after significant market rally to lock in profits.	Buy 2 350 Puts Sell 2 370 Calls	Flat Decline to 350 Increase to 370	0 0 0	0 0 0
Ratio Write	Reward equal to premium collected; high probability of profit; requires some monitoring.	Best used after significant rally to add return to portfolio.	Buy 2 360 Calls and Sell 5 370 Calls	Flat Decline to 350 Increase to 370	+850 +850 +4,350	+ 3.3% + 3.3% +16.8%

CHAPTER 5

THE OPTION TRADING PLAN

ORGANIZING YOUR PLAN

How can an option trader organize his research most effectively? This can seem quite confusing. In every market the trader is faced with three months of actively traded options containing approximately 10 actively traded strike prices each month for both puts and calls; and countless numbers of combinations and strategies that can be initiated between these options. To the new option trader, this can look like an insurmountable task. But, with proper organization and a few simple rules, order can be made out of this chaos.

First, use the process of elimination to pare down the amount of research and work that you plan to do each week. Illiquid option markets are dropped from consideration. (Any option market that does not trade an average daily volume of more than 1000 contracts.)

Second is the elimination of all but seven types of option strategies. The strategies eliminated include all of the so called arbitrage strategies including box spreads, conversions, butterflies, etc. As discussed before, although these spreads are great for floor traders and firms that specialize in arbitrage, the commissions and slippage on these trades make them economically unfeasible for everyone else. This leaves only seven positions (our "trading edge" strategies) to consider:

1. Option Purchase ("Free Trade")
2. Synthetic Futures Position
3. Neutral Option Position
4. Ratio Option Spread
5. Reverse-Ratio Spread
6. In-The-Money-Debit Spread
7. Calendar Spread

Then consider two final elements of importance—option volatility and the technical pattern of the market.

- In considering option volatility, compare current volatility readings with those of the last several weeks, months and years to both determine the trend in volatility and see whether current option volatility is relatively high, low or mediocre. High volatility readings alert us to potential option selling strategies, and with low volatility, option purchases should be considered.

- Finally, review the technical pattern of the market to determine whether there is any recognizable chart pattern that has been reliable in the past. Look at the short, intermediate, and long-term trends, and support and resistance levels.

You can then combine these factors to use the benefits of option strategies with the most reliable chart patterns. There is no denying that option strategies are initially more work than trading only futures; however, the benefits and advantages of option strategies which are unavailable anywhere else (taking advantage of under- and over-valued options, the time-value decay of options, and using neutral positions for flat markets) can be very effective for the knowledgeable option trader.

GETTING A TRADING EDGE OVER THE MARKET

Without a plan and the discipline to follow it, even the best trader or system is destined to lose. This is the case in options trading, the same as it is in everyday business.

There have been many instances of successful companies failing because of their inability to make long-term plans. This is magnified to an even greater degree when trading the markets. This is because of both the leverage factor and the short time periods in which large moves may occur. This is, of course, one of the attractions of the market—that large profits and huge returns can be made quickly; but these same factors can work against the trader who does not have a plan.

I have devised several rules that are part of my general trading plan. Although the majority of my work is directed toward using disparity in option premium to my advantage, I found that I cannot trade in a vacuum. I must know what the trend of the market is, either neutral, bullish or bearish, and must also be able to recognize chart patterns that have been reliable in the past to give me an indication of the most likely future course of the market.

My plan encompasses what I feel are the strongest points of mathematical probability, money management, system trading, and discipline. It includes the following:

1. Determination of the trend by simple trendline analysis;
2. Using technical formations that in the past have had a high degree of reliability;
3. Using strict principles of money management requiring option purchases only on pull-backs within a trend, and then to sell or hedge part of the position on significant rallies;
4. Trading on a long-term basis most of the time (where prices are more predictable);
5. Trading only in the direction of the trend;
6. Using disparities in option pricing to our advantage, as well as positions that are profitable over a wide range of prices;
7. Using neutral option positions to trade flat or choppy markets.

This system provides flexibility to take advantage of many different types of market situations. In markets that have very high option premium and great disparity in option prices, I place greater weight on Principle number 6. In contrast, in markets with reliable chart patterns, I place the strongest emphasis on Principle number 2. (However, none of these items can be ignored when taking trades; all must be considered).

Also important is the concept of risk/reward and probability of profit. Risk/reward can be determined absolutely by comparing the actual dollar risk with the profit objective. However, the probability of profit is more of an "art" and can only be estimated. In general I give all option purchases a 50% probability of profit; synthetic futures positions

50-80%; neutral option positions 75-90%; ratio and reverse-ratio spreads 65-80%. In all cases I have found as the probability of profit increases, the risk/reward ratio will decrease. For example, the risk/reward on free trades with a 50% probability of profit can be 30-1 or better; while the risk/reward of neutral positions normally is in the 4-1 range.

My guideline is that a trade should have at least a 75% probability of profit or a 10-1 risk/reward before I will consider initiating it.

ADJUSTING YOUR PLAN TO MARKET CONDITIONS

Most trading systems or technical indicators are designed with a limited number of variables by researching the action of past markets. This is because of traders perceptions that the markets are likely to behave similar to the way they have in the past. Systems are then designed that would have been profitable in previous years, with the expectation that similar action in the future will also produce successful results.

Problems occur when markets begin to act either differently than they have in the past, or when the system is not designed for the types of markets that are presently occurring. For example, a system that was designed prior to 1987 would fail to take into account the large moves that occur now after the release of government reports, particularly the monthly trade deficit figures. Therefore, the moves caused by the release of these reports or by newly active European institutional traders could cause a good position to be "stopped out" by a short term volatile move or, conversely, could cause large losses as the market flies by the traders stop-loss points.

Similarly, a system designed to trade trending markets would have a difficult time trading a flat or choppy market. This is one of the biggest problems that many systems or technical indicators have. They are non-adjusting to different market conditions.

This is a benefit that you can acquire by using option strategies. You can constantly change your strategies to fit the market, since you have strategies that work with flat markets, choppy markets, trending markets, and volatile markets. There is no need to change your trading system, only the type of trade initiated.

Therefore, you can combine many strategies to fit the individual markets, not expecting one system or method to work each market. This is, of course, more logical—as how can one expect to have the same system work equally well in volatile and non-volatile markets; and in flat or trending markets? This flexibility, being able to adjust strategies to the type of market, can provide the option strategist with a "trading edge."

COMBINING TRENDLINE AND VOLATILITY IN YOUR PLAN

Probably the first item most traders have learned is use of the trendline. The trendline is a technical indicator that determines for the trader the long, intermediate and short term direction of the market. Simply stated, a trendline is a line drawn connecting the significant high or low points on a chart. A "long" position is taken as long as the prices are above the trendline and a "neutral" position on the break to the outside of the line and a short position when a new downtrend line forms. Drawing trendlines is more of an art than a science. Exhibit 5.1 shows charts of some selected markets with their trendlines as I would draw them.

How do we put these together for use in the trading plan? In my trading plan, I look at trends over a 10 year, 2-1/2 year, 6 month, and one month period (Exhibit 5.2).

To initiate an option strategy, on the long side (converse reasoning will be used on a short side position), the one and 6 month indicator should be up. If the 2-1/2 year and 10 year trends are also in an uptrend I will take a stronger position.

I then examine volatility to determine whether the current volatility is at relatively low levels suggesting option buying strategies, or whether volatility is at a very high level in which case I would prefer ratio spreads or neutral option positions. I use these rules to initiate trades using option strategies that have the highest probability of profit by using both trendline and volatility analysis along with sound money management techniques.

There are two excellent publications that are available free that provide charts of technical pattern of the markets and historical and implied volatility. They are sent out monthly, and are available from CBOT Financial Update in care of Marketing Subscriptions, CBOT, 141 West Jackson Boulevard, Suite 2210, Chicago, Illinois 60604; and the CME Futures and Options Review in care of CME, FCM Marketing Department, Chicago, Illinois 60606 (Exhibit 5.3, 5.4, 5.5).

Exhibit 5.1
Selected Market Trendlines

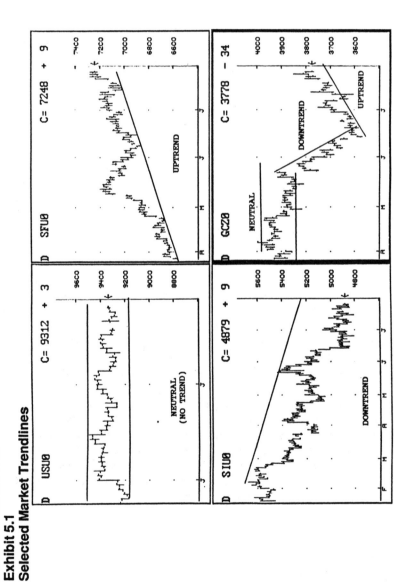

Exhibit 5.2
Gold Futures Charts of Trends

Exhibit 5.3

Exhibit 5.4

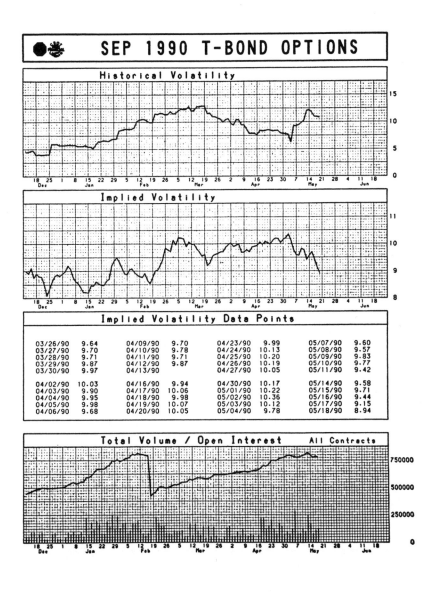

SEP 1990 T-BOND OPTIONS

Historical Volatility

Implied Volatility

Implied Volatility Data Points

03/26/90	9.64	04/09/90	9.70	04/23/90	9.99	05/07/90	9.60
03/27/90	9.70	04/10/90	9.78	04/24/90	10.13	05/08/90	9.57
03/28/90	9.71	04/11/90	9.71	04/25/90	10.20	05/09/90	9.83
03/29/90	9.87	04/12/90	9.87	04/26/90	10.19	05/10/90	9.77
03/30/90	9.97	04/13/90		04/27/90	10.05	05/11/90	9.42
04/02/90	10.03	04/16/90	9.94	04/30/90	10.17	05/14/90	9.58
04/03/90	9.90	04/17/90	10.06	05/01/90	10.22	05/15/90	9.71
04/04/90	9.95	04/18/90	9.98	05/02/90	10.36	05/16/90	9.44
04/05/90	9.98	04/19/90	10.07	05/03/90	10.12	05/17/90	9.15
04/06/90	9.68	04/20/90	10.05	05/04/90	9.78	05/18/90	8.94

Total Volume / Open Interest   All Contracts

Exhibit 5.5

USING TRADING SYSTEMS PROFITABLY

Most of us are familiar with the adage: "put an infinite number of monkeys at an infinite number of typewriters, with an infinite amount of time, and you can guarantee soon that all the great works of the world will be reproduced."

Unfortunately, from the traders standpoint, this adage also applies to advisors, newsletter writers, and system development in the markets. We have an infinite number of them, making every imaginable prediction. The trader's question is whether he is following the right monkey. Time and time again, we have all heard claims that the "Holy Grail" (perfect system) has been developed. The basis of these systems range from main-frame computer based systems to the positioning of the moon and the planets. Unfortunately, they generally all have one thing in common . . . that is, once we begin trading them, the systems lose money for us. Although 95% of the advisory services claim their market predictions are correct 95% of the time, it still seems that 95% of the public that follow these services still lose money. Why is that? There are several reasons:

First of all the system may just be no good, fraudulent or devised by "backtracking." For this reason, I recommend that you investigate very carefully any system, especially those with only a "hypothetical" track record.

Second, the system is modified by the user. Many times a person will spend a lot of money on a system, computer program, or advisory service and then decide to selectively use the trades that he likes, blended with another trading advisor's thoughts; or not take a trade because the *Wall Street Journal* indicates that the trade would probably lose. What that individual has done is produce an entirely new system, which in all probability will not be as good as the original one. Fred Gehm, in his excellent book on money management, states that even if one were to produce the perfect system and print it in the *Wall Street Journal*, it is unlikely that one out of ten traders would follow it exactly.

Although system misuse and lack of discipline as described above are major causes of losses in trading systems, the biggest cause for loss when an otherwise good system is used is poor money management. These include the following faults:

A. Systems that are developed only for entering and exiting positions, which may be excellent, but have not considered money management whatsoever.

B. Systems that are designed to trade on a short basis and fail to take into account slippage and commission charges, which can easily run 25% per year. This, on top of other costs such as charting, services, computers, and publications, can require the trader to produce a 30% return or more before he regains his initial capital each year.

C. Systems that have rules that make the trader uncomfortable can cause losses. For example, systems that require the trader to take large risks, take many consecutive losses, or trade contracts with which they are unfamiliar will eventually break down the individual's discipline and cause the trader to deviate from the system.

The final reason for system or advisor failure is not adjusting to changing market conditions. This causes a system that makes money in a trending market to lose it in a flat market; it causes many otherwise good systems to lose money in volatile markets because of their lack of recognition of these types of markets, and leads to otherwise good trades being terminated with "stops" that are too close, or cause large losses with stops that are too far away.

The following rules are designed for the better trading system:

1. **FOLLOW THE TRENDS**

2. **USE OPTION STRATEGIES THAT GIVE YOU A "TRADING EDGE"**

3. **TRADE ON A LONG TERM BASIS!**

Research, statistics and mathematical probability prove that long-term, well capitalized traders often make money, while short-term, under capitalized traders consistently lose money.

The reasoning behind this can be shown through mathematical probability. The bell shaped curves in Exhibit 5.6 provides you with the mathematical probability of gold prices during the next two years, one year, six months and 30 days. As shown, the range of prices is greater the further out in time that you go; however, percentage-wise, it is far less than the increased holding period. For example, in twelve times the

Exhibit 5.6

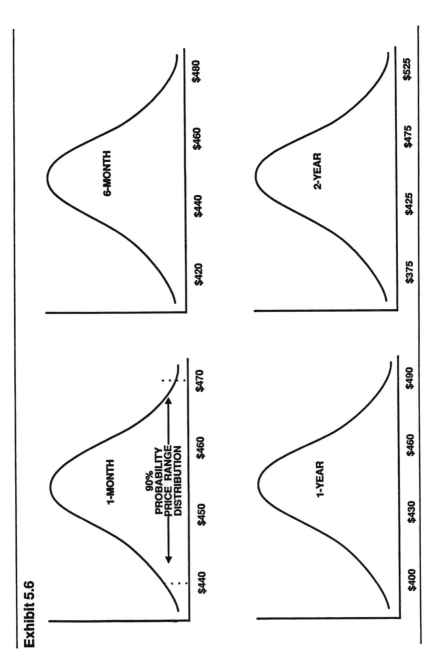

amount of time (from one month to one year) the 90% probable range of gold prices increases only three times.

This means that prices are much more volatile on a short term basis, and less predictable. It is just this volatility coupled with the great leverage available in futures and options (sometimes exceeding 98%) that can cause a small or under capitalized traders loss.

Now, let's assume that you have found a system that meets all your requirements. What you do next to maximize your chances for success is:

1. Follow it exactly without exception, until it loses a predetermined amount of your capital (20% - 50%).

2. If you lack the discipline, time, or ability to trade the system, find someone else who does to execute it for you; or

3. Have the advisor trade it for you (make sure that he also trades his own money and/or is compensated only by a percentage of profits).

The conclusion that we all want to hear, though, is—What is the bottomline? *Can you make money by boring long-term trading, "do-nothing" neutral option strategies, and the hard work involved in proper money management trading and planning?* No guarantees, of course! However, how can your trading not improve when you remove yourself from the class of traders who have been destined to lose 90% of the time because of their requirement and necessity of everything going right for them; to the professional, long-term traders arena, who use every available advantage to their benefit?

MONEY MANAGEMENT AND YOUR PLAN

Money management is another crucial, if not the most important, principle to obtaining a "trading edge."

Proper money management requires never risking more than 10% of your trading account's capital on any one position. (In fact, larger traders use even lower figures of between 2 and 5 percent. These figures may actually be better for strict money management principles; however, for smaller accounts and more aggressive traders, a 10% maximum would still be within reason on selected trades.)

Never vary from this principle. Does this mean that you can never build a large position, since you take so little risk initially? Absolutely not! You can still accumulate a large long-term position, and keep your risk within these manageable guidelines.

First, determine your risk level for every trade. Enter each trade with a certain set of principles. For example, recently I felt that bonds had broken out of a consolidation triangle and therefore recommended bullish option strategies. In determining the amount of potential loss, I have to determine what would change my mind from this reasoning. In bonds, I decided that a close under the area of the old lows would show a much weaker market than I expected when I entered into this position, and would violate my original reasons for initiating it.

Determine the options that you want to purchase by analysis of various options strategies and their benefits. In bonds, I noted that the close to expiration March options were 20% or more overvalued as compared to the June options, so calendar option spreads were constructed to take advantage of this disparity.

Next, determine what the loss level would be if the market "stopped us out." This makes it easy to determine how many positions you can afford to initiate. (I have a standard rule that I will not risk more than $500 per position, in any case, and occasionally, when I feel that there is not a great "stop-out" point, I limit my risk to either one-half of the premium of the option, or to some other arbitrary maximum amount, such as $300.)

All of these principles have one thing in common—the preservation of capital in times when positions are wrong. Limiting losses to 10% of your capital gives you at least 9 more entry points into the markets. You would have to have a very bad string of luck to quickly lose your capital using this principle. In fact, this principle gives you even more than the 10 times it seems to challenge the markets.

Assume that in your $10,000 account you are stopped-out for the maximum 10% loss each time. The first time you would lose $1,000 and your account would be worth $9,000. The second time you would lose $900 and your account would be worth $8,100, etc. You would, in fact, have 20 chances at the market before your trading capital got down to $1,000.

Now let's look at the much more exciting time when your trading decision is right and the market begins to move in your favor. Are your profits limited because you entered into too small a position in the first place instead of using all of your capital as margin? Not at all. Although some initial profits may be missed, you are a long-term trader, and most markets in a long-term trend always pull back or consolidate many times on its way to give you many chances to enter.

One trader mentioned in the book *Market Wizards* did extremely well in silver's move in 1978-1980, when silver moved from under $3 to $50. He did not enter the majority of his position at $3 or $4 or $5, or even at $7 or $8 or $10. In fact, most of his position was entered into at $15 when the trend in silver was confirmed. Then was he lucky/intelligent enough to exit silver at the top near $50? No. He got out at $30 after the uptrend had been broken, and *only* made an average of $15 or $75,000 per contract! What he did was take the easy money out of the market looking for only 50% to 60% of the trend, out of the middle, without trying to pick tops or bottoms.

How do you apply this to your trading? After entering into your initial position you should always have a profit objective and look to hedge your trades, take some profits, or turn your positions into free trades after the market moves in your favor. When your initial capital is protected and more funds are available for new positions, then look to enter into new options positions on the next reaction.

This type of trading continues as long as the trend continues. It is entirely conceivable that over a period of a year that a single position could become a 10, 20 lot or more position, never having a risk exceeding your initial amount.

By keeping your losses small when the markets don't work, you are then in a position to hit the markets hard when you are correct! Using options to get a "trading edge," being disciplined to trade only at times when the best opportunities are present, and continually following your trading plan is the essence of good trading.

CHAPTER 6

OTHER IMPORTANT OPTION TRADING PRINCIPLES

Most traders look at options as a substitute for an outright position, where you merely buy a call when you are bullish, or a put if you are bearish. However, option strategies can be used to express a more exacting view on the market and can allow you to initiate types of positions that are otherwise unavailable.

If you trade only net positions in stocks or futures, you are limited to buying the market if you are bullish, or selling it if you are bearish. Of course, you may adjust the quantity of your position or stop/loss points based on your expectation of what the market might do; but this is the extent of your latitude.

What would you do if you felt you didn't know exactly where the market was going, but felt fairly certain that it was going to maintain a certain range of prices in the near future? Suppose you felt that a market had bottomed, but you missed buying at its best prices. How would you like to be able to buy this market at less than today's price or be absolutely guaranteed a profit? What if you were bullish on the market, however you didn't want to lose if the market went slightly against you?

And finally, what if you thought the market was going to slowly move up within a limited range and you wanted a position with a high probability of profit? Wouldn't it be advantageous to have a way to initiate these exact trades?

All of these positions are available to the knowledgeable option trader. These types of positions add another benefit to the list of advantages that can be found in options.

TRADING A BULLISH MARKET WITHOUT ANY RISK OF LOSS IF THE MARKET MOVES LOWER (AGAINST YOU)

In August of 1987, silver was trading at between $7.50 and $8 after having moved from $5.50 up to almost $10 over the previous several months. At that time I was bullish but, since silver had been in a long-term down trend, I felt a position in futures or options had too much risk. However, out-of-the-money silver calls had extremely high premiums (volatility), about twice that of closer to-the-money calls. To take advantage of this disparity, I initiated ratio option spreads (buying a call, selling 2 higher calls) by purchasing the December silver $9 calls and selling 2 December silver $11.25 calls for each call purchased. I was able to receive a premium of up to $1,000 per position more for the two calls I sold, than the one I purchased.

This position had no downside risk, since, if the silver options expired with the price of silver under $9, all of the options would be worthless. (In fact, I would profit by the amount of premium I had received.) If silver moved higher, I would make $50 for every one cent silver exceeded the strike price of the options I purchased (Exhibit 6.1).

In fact, these positions would be profitable through the $14 level of silver, a price that hadn't been realized since the early 1980s. The combination of these factors made this position an excellent one - no downside potential and profits available if the market continued to move up. The only risk at all in this position was if the strike price of the options sold were exceeded, since I was short two options for every one I had purchased. (I recommend closing out the entire position if this occurs.) However, since the closest to-the-money options would gain in value much quicker then the out-of-the-money options, and the out-of-the-money options would deteriorate in time value faster, this position would continue to work in my favor in most instances.

Exhibit 6.1
Profit/Loss of December Silver Ratio Spread

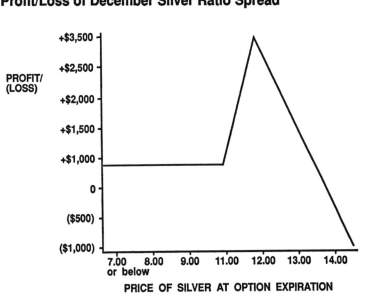

PROFIT/
(LOSS)

PRICE OF SILVER AT OPTION EXPIRATION

Buying A Market At Less Than Today's Price

In early 1991, when silver plunged to near $3.50 per ounce, some bullish investors thought it was an excellent time to purchase silver, while others wanted to wait until it was even lower. There was, in fact, a way that you could satisfy both of these views by purchasing silver at $3.75 or receiving a return that would be over 50% annually.

You could sell a July $3.00 put option and receive a premium of $300. Since the maintenance margin required for this strategy was $1,000, this would produce a return of 30% (or 90% annually) if, when this option expired the contract was above $3.00. This is because no purchaser of a $3.00 put would want to exercise this option, since they can sell silver at a higher price through the cash or futures market. Therefore, if silver expired above $3.00 this $300 premium was yours to keep when the silver option expired in four months, thereby producing a return of 90% per annum.

Once this put option expired, you could then proceed to the next active trading month, and again initiate this strategy. However, if silver fell to $3.00 or below and the purchaser of the $3.00 put option exercises the put, you would own silver at $3.00 per ounce less the $300 premium or 6 cents per ounce that you were paid for this put, an effective price of $2.94 per ounce for your silver. Since silver was trading at $3.50 per ounce when you initiated this strategy, you would be purchasing silver for 50 cents less than its previous price, a savings of more than 10%.

This strategy works similarly for any listed stock or commodity. However, this is for the long-term investor who has made a decision that he wants to purchase the stock or commodity at a lower price. This is because if the market continues to move lower, a trader will experience losses (in this case, below $2.94). And, although profits will be made if the market moves higher, you will not be "in the market" if a large move begins to occur. However, not withstanding these two situations, it is an excellent strategy to lower your ownership costs or obtain a high return in almost any market.

Exhibit 6.2
Profit/Loss

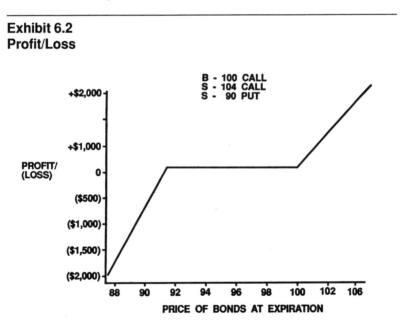

MARKET VIEWS—TRADING RANGE TO SLIGHTLY BULLISH

At the end of September 1989, bonds were maintaining a wide range between the 94 and 98 area, after previously rallying to the 100 level early in the month. My market view was long-term bullish; however, it looked like an intermediate top was in place that could last for several months. Therefore, I recommended buying the March bond 100 call and selling the 90 put and 104 call. By doing this, the price of the options I sold were paying for the call I purchased. The position would not lose money unless bonds went below the 90 level. However, since there was unlimited loss if this did occur, and it was my view in entering the trade that bonds would not go below the 94 level, I was using a close under 9400 as my signal to exit this trade. This would have produced a loss of approximately $300, depending on how quickly this occurred. (On the upside, my profit objective was $4,000, producing a position that had a risk/reward of 10 to 1 as shown in Exhibit 6.2.)

PROFITING FROM AN OPTION POSITION WHEN YOU DON'T KNOW WHERE THE MARKET IS GOING, BUT FEEL THAT YOU KNOW WHERE IT *ISN'T* GOING

There are two positions that can reflect your views on the market in these instances: the synthetic futures position and the neutral option strategy.

In late 1985, the S&P had been in a bull market for almost two years; however, it had been languishing at the 170 to 180 level most of the year. At that time, I wasn't certain that a large rally would occur (even though it subsequently did); however, I was confident that the 170 level would hold. Therefore, with the market trading at about 180, I was able to purchase a December S&P 195 call and sell the 170 put and receive a credit (*synthetic futures position*). This meant that as long as the market stayed above 170 (my view of the market), I would profit on the transaction. And, if the market did rally strongly, I would not only have a call that didn't cost me anything, but also had the potential for unlimited profits above the 195 level.

At the beginning of 1988, bonds were trading at the 90 level, and it was my view that I would see a range in the next several months between 80 and 100. Option premium was also at historically high levels at that time, allowing me to sell 80 puts and 100 calls (*neutral option*

Exhibit 6.3
Profit/Loss of Neutral Option Position

PRICE OF BONDS AT OPTION EXPIRATION

---

position) for up to $1,000. Since these options would expire worthless in less than six months if bonds stayed within this large 20 point range, I would receive a return of almost 50% on margin (100% annualized) without having to predict market direction (Exhibit 6.3).

These examples show some of the circumstances that provide another benefit of option strategies—being able to profit by only knowing where the market *isn't* going.

ARE OPTION PUT AND CALL PRICES, RATIO, OR VOLUME PREDICTIVE OF MARKET DIRECTION?

Changes In Option Premium Levels

Option premium levels are determined by the volatility in the particular market. Quite simply, if a market is not making significant moves in either direction, option premium should be low, as buyers of options would not be willing to pay much for an option that has little expectation of value due to the inactive market. Option sellers would also feel more comfortable selling options in this type of market, and would be content with less premium than usual.

In a very active market, option sellers will refuse to sell options unless a high premium is received because of the unlimited risk of loss if the market moves against them. Also, option buyers would be willing to pay more for their purchases, which now have a higher probability of value.

The differences in option premium levels can be quite dramatic. For example, at the end of September 1989, with option premium near historical low levels in silver, I could purchase the March silver 575 call, the closest to-the-money option for $650. This option was only one strike price (25 cents) out-of-the-money and had almost five months before expiration. However, in 1987 when silver rallied quickly from $6 to $8 and volatility increased dramatically, I was able to sell $11.25 silver calls, options that were over 10 strike prices from the money ($3) for up to $2,000!

Most of the time, the change in option premium levels is not an advance indicator of what's likely to happen, but only mirrors the changes in the futures prices. Rarely are these changes in advance, providing any predictive value. And even when they do lead the market action, the changes are very subtle.

For example, prior to the 20 point break in bond prices from the 100 level in 1987, I noticed the premium on bond puts increasing around 20%, without any significant market action. Volatility was at that time close to historically low levels. This increase in volatility seemed to reflect the fact that large traders (professionals, hedgers, institutions) were entering the market, either speculatively, or to hedge their previously profitable positions. This increase in volatility was significant, because bond options are much more liquid than any other option contract, and the typical bond option trader is a more sophisticated investor. There are few incidents similar to this, and the changes are usually so subtle, that unless you have been watching the market closely, they will be missed by most traders.

CHANGES IN PUT AND CALL RATIOS OR VOLUME

After studying changes in put and call ratios and volume of options traded over the last several years in many different option contracts, I have been unable to find any correlation that would help to accurately predict future price action. The reason for this is that options are still in their infancy and are in the process of being "discovered" by many institutional traders. Many times the increase in volume in option contracts can be tied solely to the fact that more traders are now beginning to use options.

Another reason that this indicator can be inaccurate is that options can be used for many different purposes. A large trader who is bullish bonds may purchase 1000 bond calls to profit from this expected move. However, another trader who is equally bullish bonds, but who may be long the futures or cash bonds may sell 1000 bond options just to hedge this position and lock in a rate of return with which he is comfortable.

Therefore, with the many different types of trading objectives by those in the marketplace, there is usually no mathematical significance in the increase in volume or changes in put and call ratios.

HOW OPTION STRATEGIES CAN HELP OVERCOME THE HIDDEN FACTORS THAT CAUSE LOSSES IN TRADING

Making money is, of course, everyone's objective in trading. This is where you should place the emphasis of your time. Concentrate on the elements that can assist you in realizing this objective and, conversely, prevent and discard elements that interfere with your moneymaking objective.

Does buying these expensive, complicated systems, learning the intricacies of market behavior, and even option strategies, provide the basis for a profitable trading plan? More often than not, the answer to this question is no. This is because of several hidden factors that most traders overlook.

1.   *The Hidden Emotional Factors in Trading*

Although fear, greed, and the lack of discipline are frequently discussed, two overlooked, often ignored subjects are "over-trading" (including failing to take breaks from trading for the necessary "rest and recreation" to "recharge one's batteries"), and only trading when situations present you with trades that have the highest probability of profit (either because of the markets technical pattern or disparity in option pricing).

Violation of these concepts is responsible for losses as much as any of the so called important items such as trade timing, failure to pick market direction and money management.

Traders are always very reluctant to be away from the markets; they do not want to miss any trading opportunities. However, with more than 30 markets that have options, each containing at least three months of option expirations and 10 or more strike prices, all in various configurations from bullish to bearish to neutral-choppy, flat, volatile, etc., enough opportunities for profitable trading will continue to occur, keeping even the most nimble trader very busy.

Traders are in battle every day with these markets, which can be very tiring and draining. After long stretches of trading, especially ones that have not been particularly rewarding, traders begin to act like "brainwashed" prisoners of war. They are ready to follow any system or pronouncement that promises profit and abandon all of their old trading methods. Instead of abandoning past work, it would be much more beneficial to take time out to examine previous errors and learn from them.

2.   *The Hidden Costs in Trading*

We have all heard that:

A.   Trading is a zero sum game.

B.   For every winner there's a loser.

C.   An average trader breaks even.

Unfortunately, these hypothesis are all wrong. As discussed in the introduction, this is because the trader, through commission, pays the salaries of all the brokers, brokerage firm personnel, all of the exchange personnel, from the floor runners to the receptionist, and all the regulatory agencies and their employees. On top of this, the trader must pay for his chart services, publications, computer, phone, etc. These fees can total over 20% of an active trader's account. This means the trader must actually profit in his trading by that amount just to break even. Even Las Vegas casinos give their customers better odds!

What it really takes to make money trading is:

1.   Making correct calls on the market (Market Prediction).

2.   Having an appropriate plan that incorporates principles of money management (Trading Plan).

3. Preservation of capital during those times when trading becomes difficult and your calls become faulty (Money Management).

Protection from loss is one advantage of using option strategies.
The reason for this is that many of the strategies are profitable over a
wide range of futures prices, and some strategies allows you to break
even or sometimes profit when you are incorrect with your market predictions.

How do you do this with option strategies? There are several positions that allow you these benefits and flexibility:

1. Synthetic Futures Positions (Option sold pays for option purchased).
2. Ratio Option Spreads (Profitable over a wide price range).
3. "Free Trades" (After completed, requires no margin and has no
loss potential).
4. Neutral Option Strategies (Only positions that profit in flat or
choppy markets).
5. Money Management Techniques with Options (Hedging futures or options positions).

Assuming that a market can move in five different ways:

1. Slowly lower,
2. Suddenly lower,
3. Neutral,
4. Slowly higher, or
5. Suddenly higher.

Most of the above strategies will be profitable if the market moves
in any 4 out of 5 of the possible ways. This can be expressed as an 80%
probability of profit.

Additionally, there are certain characteristics inherent in options
that can provide the trader with valuable advantages including:

1. Buying under-valued options;
2. Selling over-valued options;
3. Combining the sale of over-valued with the purchase of under-
valued options, allowing you to use the disparity of option
pricing to get a "trading edge";

4. Using factors of option volatility in your favor;
5. Using the time decay of options in your favor;
6. Using the limited risk functions of options in your favor.

Remember your objective is to make money, keeping it simple can perhaps be the biggest benefit and the most overlooked secret in trading.

USING OPTIONS PRIOR TO THE RELEASE OF SIGNIFICANT REPORTS OR EVENTS

As all traders are aware, the release of any major report, figures, governmental meeting and potential raising or lowering of discount rate often cause large moves in the markets when the actual figure is different than the one expected.

Therefore, knowing the basic information regarding these reports is essential for all traders so that you can, at least, assess the potential for such a move. Additionally, when a report comes out significantly different than expected, you will want to observe the markets' reaction to the report. In fact, I feel that this is the most important indicator of the markets strength or weakness. For example, when an unexpectedly favorable report fails to cause any significant move in the market, the market may be "tired" and you should be cautious about initiating new positions.

In 1984 and 1985, the markets eagerly awaited the money supply figures on Thursday evenings which would then significantly effect the metals markets and, to a lesser degree, the stock and financial markets. In 1987-88, the trade deficit figure resulted in major moves in the currencies, causing 300-400 point ranges in the Swiss Franc and Japanese Yen in a matter of minutes. The movement in the currency market then spilled over into other markets, thereby affecting their action also. Anticipated raising and lowering of the discount rate has also caused similar reactions in the financial and S&P 500 markets. Finally, the agricultural and livestock markets are greatly influenced by the release of government reports and figures.

Markets are also affected based on a government's or entity nonaction after a report. For example, in the last week of December 1987, the currency markets rose substantially when the foreign governments failed to support the dollar after a G-5 meeting. The traders took this to mean that they had decided not to support the dollar; this non-action was interpreted bearishly for the U.S. dollar. However, the governments had actually agreed to support the dollar but decided to wait until after the first of the year based on either the holiday time period, or for whatever reasons that suited their purpose.

There is, however, a major difference between the actions of the futures and options markets, both before and after these events. Prior to the release of government reports, the futures markets become quite stagnant; then become most volatile right after the release of the report, stabilizing shortly thereafter. The option markets act quite differently. Instead of stabilizing in price before a report based on the non-action in the futures market, option volatility and premium rise rapidly, peaking during the last hour of trading prior to the report. After the report is released, option pricing becomes random until the true market direction is shown, usually in the first hour after the report. However, due to the thinness of the markets and the tendency of option sellers to wait to determine the velocity of the move, it is difficult to buy options at a reasonable price until the market has stabilized (Exhibit 6.4).

Another difference between options and futures is that the out-of-the-money options increase greatly in value prior to the report. Then,

---

Exhibit 6.4
Relative Volatility Levels of Swiss Franc Options and Futures
(Before and after February 1988 Trade Deficit report. 0 = Lowest volatility level;
100 = Highest.)

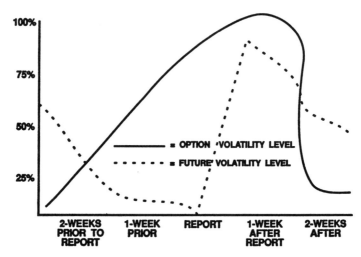

after the report is issued, and it is determined that these options are still out-of-the-money, they lose their value even quicker.

An example of this is an April Swiss Franc neutral option position that initiated one day before the February 1990 trade deficit report. At that time, a premium of $1,000 was available for selling a far out-of-the-money put and call. After the report, although the Swiss Franc had moved 100 points lower, the put had gained only 5 points in value where the call had lost 27 points in value for a net gain of 22 points or $275.

This position was attractive because computer analysis showed that a move of 200 points in either direction on the day of the report would not have caused a loss in this position (Exhibit 6.5).

I used computer evaluations of option prices to determine which options had the greatest overvaluation. These trade sheets were compiled several days before the U.S. trade deficit report which caused severe overvaluation of the Swiss Franc options. Based on this, with the contract at 7300, you could initiate neutral option positions in the April

---

Exhibit 6.5
Computer Evaluation of Option Prices

SFJ - SWISS-FRANK - APR
VOLATILITY = 14.82%   DAYS OUT = 53
INTEREST RATE = 6.50%   2-16-88

| | ********CALLS******** | | |
	76	77	78
70.00	.14	.08	.05
70.25	.16	.09	.06
70.50	.18	.11	.06
70.75	.20	.13	.08
71.00	.23	.14	.09
71.25	.26	.16	.10
71.50	.30	.19	.12
71.75	.34	.21	.13
72.00	.38	.24	.15
72.25	.42	.27	.17

| | ********CALLS******** | | |
	76	77	78
72.50	.47	.31	.20
72.75	.53	.35	.22
73.00	.58	.39	.25
73.25	.65	.44	.29
73.50	.72	.49	.32
73.75	.79	.54	.36
74.00	.87	.60	.41

SFJ - SWISS-FRANK - APR
VOLATILITY = 14.82%   DAYS OUT = 53
INTEREST RATE = 6.50%   2-16-8

| | *******PUTS********* | | |
	68	69	70
70.00	.75	1.10	1.56
70.25	.68	1.01	1.44
70.50	.61	.92	1.33
70.75	.55	.84	1.22
71.00	.50	.77	1.12
71.25	.45	.69	1.03
71.50	.40	.63	.94
71.75	.36	.57	.86
72.00	.32	.51	.78
72.25	.28	.46	.71

| | *******PUTS********* | | |
	68	69	70
72.50	.25	.41	.65
72.75	.22	.37	.59
73.00	.20	.33	.53
73.25	.17	.30	.48
73.50	.15	.26	.43
73.75	.14	.23	.39
74.00	.12	.21	.35

Source: COM-TECH SOFTWARE, 141 W. Jackson Blvd., Suite 1531-A, Chicago, IL.

Swiss Franc 69 put and 78 call at a total premium of 80 points ($1,000). Its fair value was computed at 58 ($625). Our computer evaluation showed that this position would not lose money, if the futures moved 250 points in either direction. One week later, as volatility subsided and premiums dropped for both puts and calls, this combination was trading at 36 points ($400) for a profit of $600.

While option traders had this 400 point "window" of profit, futures traders were having a much more difficult time. Shortly before the report was issued, the Swiss Franc moved up 100 points potentially "stopping-out" many short future traders. Then the market plummeted 300 points immediately thereafter, then attacking those holding long futures' positions.

This type of action also occurred before and after January's trade report. Out-of-the-money calls that became substantially over-valued the day before the report, were almost totally worthless the next day. Even the out-of-the-money puts gained very little in value, in spite of the fact that the market made a move of over 200 points lower that day.

Therefore, selling options in these instances can produce trades with high probabilities of profits. However, there are going to be times where you have a view of market direction, and want to consider buying options to profit from those expectations, so that it is not necessary to take the unlimited risk associated with future trades.

As seen in the examples above, purchasing out-of-the-money options close to reports can provide you with a trade that moves in the direction you predicted, and that may still only be slightly profitable, if at all. However, purchasing an option approximately one week prior to a report allows you to obtain a more fairly valued option. I would recommend purchasing an option at-the-money or no more than one strike price out-of-the-money, as these options are usually the most fairly valued, and responsive to a move in your favor.

The month that should be purchased is also of significance. If a longer term trade is anticipated, I would recommend an option of between three and six months duration. If one is purchasing an option just to take advantage of the report, the closest to expiration option is recommended. This option will have the largest percentage move if the report is favorable to your position. (However, this will also lose the most premium if you have guessed wrong.) Traders caught between these two dilemmas would be advised to purchase an option between two and three months in duration to combine the effects of both of these circumstances.

There are several reports in addition to the Trade Deficit report that traders watch:

1. *The Gross National Product:* This report is a broad measure of the United States economic activity. A positive number causes commentators to indicate that economic growth is expanding and the economy is healthy. This may also indicate the potential for inflation and may cause traders to perceive higher interest rates, metals prices, and potential for a weaker dollar.

2. *Unemployment Report:* This report by the Labor Department indicates whether industry is weak or strong by the number of jobs it is creating. A low number implies that there is a potential for inflation and strong economy as more people are employed and more money available in the economy.

3. *Consumer Price Index:* The Consumer Price Index is also issued by the Labor Department and reports prices for finished goods. A high CPI number indicates the potential for inflation; however, the number should be watched for seasonal variances and temporary aberrations that can cause faulty interpretation of otherwise reasonable figures.

4. *Producer Price Index:* This report is similar to the CPI; however, it measures only wholesale prices. It is important because it is released several days before the CPI and, therefore, gives a hint to the CPI's future direction.

Other reports whose names are self-descriptive of what they indicate and are interpreted similarly to the previous reports are the Index of Leading Economic Indicators, Consumer Spending, Factory Orders, Industrial Production, and Factory Capacity Utilization.

Exhibit 6.6, prepared by the Chicago Board of Trade, provides a concise summary of these reports and their possible effect on the markets.

PRICE ACTION AFTER AN IMPORTANT ECONOMIC REPORT

When I began trading in the early 1980s, I was told to "Buy the rumor, sell the fact." What this meant was before the news item was released it could be an important factor that would cause the market to move; however, after its release, it was "in the market" and already discounted.

Exhibit 6.6
Reports That Indicate Effect on Markets

Report		Effect
Consumer Price Index Rises	▼	Indicates rising inflation.
Durable Goods Orders Rise	▼	Pickup in business activity usually leads to increased credit demand.
Gross National Product Falls	▲	Reflects a slowing economy. Fed may loosen money supply, prompting a decline in interest rates.
Housing Starts Rise	▼	Shows growth in economy and increased credit demand. Fed less accommodating and may attempt tightening by allowing rates to rise.
Industrial Production Falls	▲	Indicates slowing economic growth. Fed may be more accommodating in allowing interest rates to fall to stimulate the economy.
Inventories Up	▲	Indicates a slowing economy since sales are not keeping up with production.
Leading Indicators Up	▼	Signals strength in the economy leading to greater credit demand.
Oil Prices Fall	▲	Reduces upward pressure on interest rates, thereby enhancing prices of debt securities.
Personal Income Rises	▼	The higher personal income, the more is consumed prompting increased demand and higher prices for consumer goods.
Precious Metals Prices Fall	▲	Reflects decreased inflation. Demand for inflation hedges abates.
Producer Price Index Rises	▼	Indicates rising inflation. Demand for goods rises as well as prices. Investors require higher rates of return, pushing rates up.
Retail Sales Rise	▼	Indicates stronger economic growth. Fed may have to tighten.
Unemployment Rises	▲	Indicates slow economic growth. Fed may ease credit, causing rates to drop.

I found that even a report that was favorable to a particular market would cause little movement, and often a set-back would occur, as this information was already expected, and perhaps disappointing to traders who were hoping for a more bullish report. In fact, only if a report came out much better than expected was the market favorably affected.

The markets reaction to major reports can vary so widely because of the emotion involved in making quick decisions, that traders should not attach major significance to that one day's reaction. Only when the report differs substantially from what is expected and the market fails to react, or if the market makes a significant reaction on an otherwise neutral report, should you become concerned. It is also my view, that these reports exaggerate the movement of the market by giving the traders an excuse to propel the market in the direction it was already headed.

Another difference is that, in the past, traders were more anxious to anticipate the information contained in the report. It seems that many times the large traders were correct about this information (either a good guess or advance knowledge). However, over the last few years, there seems to be less anticipation and more waiting for the actual report to be released. Then, the action begins to unfold.

RELATIONSHIPS BETWEEN THE MARKETS

In 1983, when I first began studying the possible importance of relationships between markets, the most widely watched relationships were between financial instruments and the foreign currencies. They were seemingly locked together; if United States interest rates were to rise, so would the dollar almost without fail. Another steady relationship at that time was between gold and silver which were supposed to rise and fall on a 50-1 ratio.

Finally, the relationship between the currencies and the metals was also well established. The philosophy was that if the foreign currencies were rising it was because of inflation in this country and, therefore, a good reason for strength in the precious metals as well.

What most commentators failed to consider was that just because of mathematical probability with over 30 trading markets some of them will have similar patterns quite often. In fact, there can even seem to be correlations between unrelated markets that have no fundamental basis for the relationships. Probability shows that if you have 30 people in a room, the odds are better than 50% that two of them will have exactly the same birthday, seemingly a 12 to 1 shot. With over 30 futures markets, similar unrelated relationships will continually seem to be occurring. You must weed out these unrelated situations and determine whether any true relationships do exist, to the point that they can be relied on in your trading.

Let's look into the potential relationships between the most significant market groups to determine whether any basis occurs for their interrelation.

1. Interest Rates and Foreign Currencies

In 1983 this was one of the most relied on relationship. And with good reason. As can be seen from the accompanying chart from 1983 through the middle of 1984, foreign currencies and bonds moved down in tandem. When bonds reversed in 1984, the currencies failed to follow for about six months. However, commencing in early 1985 through the middle of 1986, they then proceeded to move up in tandem (Exhibit 6.7).

From this point on, divergence occurred. Although the foreign currencies continued to move higher through the end of 1988, bonds first consolidated during 1986 before plunging during the first nine months of 1987, only correcting after the crash in October of 1987. Then, while the foreign currencies continued to move lower for the last 18 months from the beginning of 1988, bonds first consolidated and then rallied in 1989.

Is there any substance to a relationship in these markets? There is very little. First, the basis for the original relationship was that if U.S. interest rates were rising the dollar should be safer and attract more foreign investors. This fails to take into account the potential for differences between U.S. and foreign interest rates, focusing only on the changes in our country or fundamental strengths or problems within the various countries.

My conclusion, therefore, is that while the strength of the dollar may be at times important in affecting the course of interest rates, and conversely United States interest rates will always affect dollar foreign currencies exchange rates, one must not consider that the markets will have to move either opposite to or in tandem with each other.

2. Metals and the Foreign Currencies

Some correlation can be seen between the foreign currencies and gold. In the charts of gold and the Swiss Franc (Exhibit 6.8), we can see the markets rising in tandem in the late 1970s, falling together from 1980 to

Exhibit 6.7

Exhibit 6.8

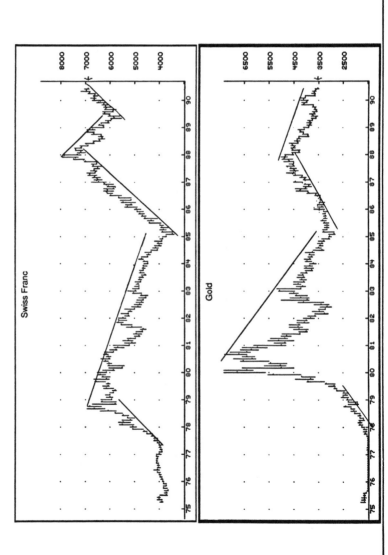

1985, rising from 1985 through 1988, and then failing from that time until the beginning of 1989. From that time to the present, the markets have diverged with Swiss Franc moving higher and gold lower.

A fundamental basis exists for this relationship; as the dollar erodes in value, its purchasing power in terms of the international commodity of gold is lessened; and conversely as its value increases, more gold can be purchased for the same dollar.

However, there is currently no valid relationship between these markets. Not only are the major turning points of the markets different, as a more emotional market can move substantially higher (or lower) and turn 3 to 18 months later, but there are also different forces at work in each market.

For example, in 1990 gold was being pushed lower partly because of cash needs by oil producing countries and the Soviet Union, which has no effect on the Swiss Franc.

3. Interest Rates and Metals

The common view that I often heard when I began trading was that higher interest rates would lead to higher precious metal prices. Higher interest rates are caused by an inflationary environment which also will cause the metals to rise; with lower interest rates there is little reason for people to invest in gold that has no return.

Currently, the view is that with the trend toward lower U.S. interest rates there is little reason for the metals to rise. However, the past history of the relationship between these markets provides little basis for these conclusions (Exhibit 6.9).

As can be seen from the charts, as bonds dropped from 1978 to 1982 (thereby denoting rising U.S. interest rates), gold prices alternately rose from 1978 to 1980 then dropped from 1980 to 1982. The markets did seemingly move in tandem from 1982 through 1986; however, this relationship began to diverge in the middle of 1986 with gold continuing to rise through the end of 1987. Then the reverse occurred; gold dropped and bonds rose.

These markets illustrate another rule. That is, it depends what set of economic principles are then governing them, as to what the relationship will be. Depending on the economic circumstances, gold and bonds can either rise and fall at the same time or act exactly opposite to each other. It is, of course, important to know which is occurring. Many times the true state of economic facts are not evident for a long time after the

Exhibit 6.9
Interest Rates (Treasury Bonds, Gold)

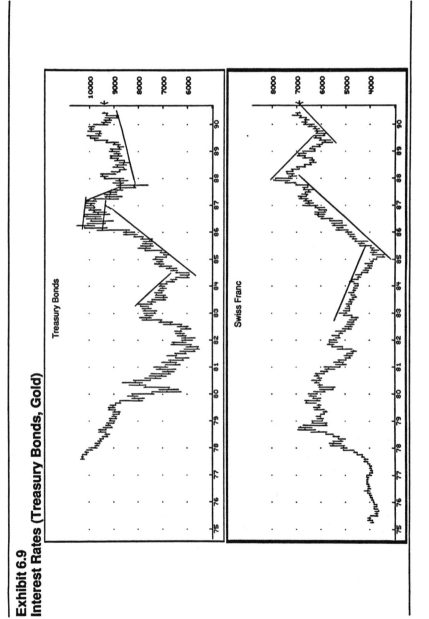

market turns. You certainly do not want to be operating under a faulty set of principles during this period.

4. Interest Rates and Stock Market

Today, one of the most followed relationships is that between the interest rates and the stock market. It is universally concluded that as interest rates continue to fall this will be supportive the stock market. Conversely, higher rates would be damaging as people would move their money into interest rate sensitive instruments if rates increase and out of the stock market.

Although this relationship has worked well from September 1990 to April 1991, and also from June 1984 to June 1986, when both markets moved in tandem, this has not always been the case. In fact from March of 1988 the reverse occurred, with interest rates moving higher along with the stock market. This also occurred in 1982 through 1985 when the S&P bottomed and then rose over 50% during this period while interest rates increased about almost the same amount. This also occurred between July of 1986 and September 1987. During the stock market crash of 1987, rates dropped substantially as investors moved from the markets to bonds (Exhibit 6.10). Therefore, similar to the relationship between gold and interest rates, this one also depends on the current economic environment.

5. Other Markets

The agricultural markets seem to move in tandem only during severe drought or weather problem markets which affect all of the agricultural commodities together. Also, strong evidence of inflation or recession has caused these markets to move together in the past. Otherwise, prices are determined by normal supply and demand factors for the individual markets.

Little relationship seems to occur in the soft commodities as can be seen recently with sugar trading at 7 years highs while cocoa fell to 14 year lows at the same time.

In the livestock sector, little current relationship can be also seen between pork bellies and live hogs. Although in the past they have many times moved in the same direction, they now have had little correlation as pork bellies have declined in value by over 50% the last two years while live hogs have traded in range during the last year and a half.

Exhibit 6.10
Interest Rates and the Stock Market (Treasury Bonds and S&P 500)

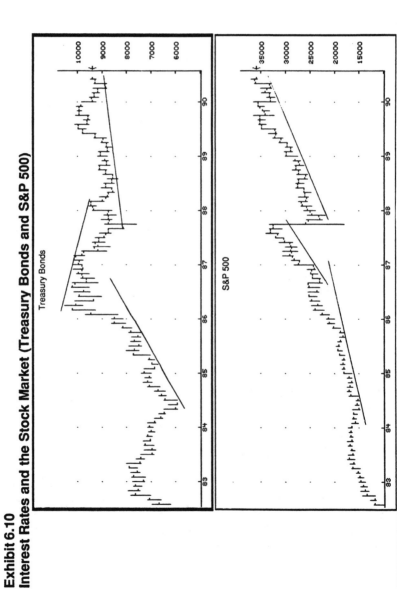

Similar distinction can be made between live cattle and live hogs which have moved in opposite directions for the last three years and show no correlation previous to this time.

Currently our economy points to no positive correlation between any markets. However, as economic conditions change, underlying relationships can also change, so it is recommended that relationships between markets be constantly monitored.

INTERPRETING WEEKLY OPTION STATISTICS

Although many books have been written providing the mathematical basis for option valuation, little has been written on the practical nature of how to actually profit in real-time trading.

Further, I know of no book or publication that has been written on how options may react differently at times to various movements in the underlying futures market. It is the premise of all writers that if the market moves up—calls gain in value, and if the market moves down— puts increase. This simple premise, although usually correct during a single trading day, provides the basis for many losses in option trading.

Since I like to concentrate on finding disparity in option pricing, the right strategies to initiate, and the most opportune times to initiate them, I feel it is important to view how each option, strike price, and month reacts in relationship to the movement of the futures market.

Previously, one problem in studying this relationship was the failure of being able to obtain this information from a readily available publication. Although this information is available to floor traders on various exchanges, it is difficult for us "off-floor" traders to obtain and assimilate this information from each individual exchange. However, *Barron's* has begun reporting the high/low, net change, volume and open interest for the week for almost all the strike prices of future/options. You will find it enlightening to note the net change of an option at the end of the week after all the movement and emotion during those five days have been removed.

For example, although treasury bonds moved up and down almost half a point a day during a week, the futures ended the week little changed. However, most of the out-of-the-money calls and puts lost value. This was because this directionless type of movement allows the natural time value decay of option premium to accelerate and causes premium to drop.

On the other hand, during the same week the upward movement in the currencies caused volatility to rise, with calls moving up in value and puts losing only little of their premium (Exhibit 6.11).

One final aspect to consider is the open interest for each individual option strike price. You may find that some of the options have a relatively small open interest. This does not concern me for several reasons. First of all, if I cannot close out a position because of either inadequate volume or too much slippage, I can always temporarily hedge with another strike price or month or even a futures contract. (However, I don't remember a time when this was ever necessary.)

Secondly, it is generally the far out-of-the-money options (that I have sold) that are the most illiquid. If these options remain out-of-the-money and stay illiquid, I have little concern, as I am profiting by the time value decay and can merely choose to allow the option to expire as worthless. However, if the futures began to approach the strike price of the option sold, this option always becomes more liquid, and easier to liquidate, if necessary.

Studying these charts for one hour each weekend can provide a trader with invaluable information and insight.

INTEGRATING OPTIONS INTO YOUR FUTURES TRADING PLAN

If you are successful trader, I would not suggest that you abandon your current trading plan or methods and trade options only. But, by integrating options at opportune times with your trading, your probability of profit could be substantially increased.

However, if your trading has been only marginally successful or unprofitable, I would strongly suggest that you look either at trading options exclusively or at least integrating options trading into your plan.

The following methods can be most useful for integrating options into a futures trading plan:

1.   Using an Option Instead of a Stop to Protect a Contract

Purchasing an option for protection will allow a trader to hold a contract with a greatly reduced risk. This is a significantly better way to protect a position instead of placing a stop in the market, which could be hit on a sudden reaction as the trader watches in horror as his stop is hit at close to the low of the entire move. In a situation such as this, the cost of this

Exhibit 6.11
Option Statistics: Swiss Franc and Treasury Bonds

Month Strike Vol Int High Low Sett PtChg Future Sett

Swiss Franc

Month	Strike	Vol	Int	High	Low	Sett	PtChg	Future Sett
			S-FRANC CALL					
APR	88	71	25	172	—	3.04	+ 107	.7401
APR	88	72	143	885	2.15	1.05	2.09 + 97	.7401
APR	88	73	428	788	1.36	.40	1.22 + 70	.7401
APR	88	74	3020	2708	.65	.18	.56 + 34	.7401
APR	88	75	295	718	.29	.06	.22 + 12	.7401
APR	88	76	113	188	.12	.07	.09 + 4	.7401
APR	88	77	5	163	.03	.02	.05 + 2	.7401
APR	88	78	1	183	.02	—	.03 + 1	.7401
APR	88	79		74	—	—	.01	.7401
APR	88	80		2	—	—	CAB - 1	.7401
APR	88	81		2	—	—	CAB - 1	.7401
MAY	88	72		313	2.45	—	2.40 + 83	.7401
MAY	88	73	85	142	1.75	—	1.68 + 67	.7401
MAY	88	74	190	456	1.17	.60	1.13 + 52	.7401
MAY	88	75	145	155	.80	.35	.73 + 38	.7401
MAY	88	76	22	50	.48	.22	.46 + 26	.7401
MAY	88	77		1	.28	—	.28 + 16	.7401
JUN	88	67		357	—	—	6.95 + 108	.7401
JUN	88	68		126	—	—	6.01 + 106	.7401
JUN	88	69		176	—	—	5.10 + 103	.7401
JUN	88	70	7	66	4.20	3.25	4.23 + 98	.7401
JUN	88	71	1	510	3.52	2.57	3.41 + 90	.7401
JUN	88	72	42	514	2.76	1.75	2.67 + 78	.7401
JUN	88	73	612	2889	2.10	1.24	2.02 + 66	.7401
JUN	88	74	743	1398	1.60	.92	1.48 + 53	.7401
JUN	88	75	173	779	1.18	.60	1.07 + 42	.7401
JUN	88	76	282	914	.82	.44	.75 + 32	.7401
JUN	88	77	488	676	.60	.28	.52 + 23	.7401
JUN	88	78	13	288	.42	.19	.36 + 16	.7401
JUN	88	79	36	221	.27	.15	.25 + 10	.7401
JUN	88	80		360	.17	—	.17 + 7	.7401
JUN	88	81		37	—	—	.11 + 4	.7401
JUN	88	82		72	—	—	.08 + 3	.7401
JUN	88	83		38	.04	—	.05 + 3	.7401
JUN	88	84		12	—	—	.02 + 1	.7401
SEP	88	70		3	—	—	5.55 + 89	.7494
SEP	88	72		150	—	—	4.79 + 81	.7494
SEP	88	73		627	3.43	—	3.45 + 68	.7494
SEP	88	74	260	738	2.90	—	2.87 + 60	.7494
SEP	88	75		102	2.40	1.85	2.38 + 53	.7494
SEP	88	76	4	21	2.09	1.51	1.97 + 47	.7494
SEP	88	77	1	514	1.65	—	1.61 + 41	.7494
SEP	88	78	22	340	1.35	—	1.31 + 36	.7494
SEP	88	79	1	804	1.05	—	1.05 + 30	.7494
SEP	88	80		153	.87	—	.84 + 25	.7494
SEP	88	81	1	37	.67	—	.67 + 21	.7494
SEP	88	82	21	55	.48	—	.53 + 17	.7494
SEP	88	83	1	2	.38	—	.42 + 14	.7494
SEP	88	84	1	22	.38	—	.32 + 9	.7494
DEC	88	73		50	—	—	4.68 + 85	.7593
DEC	88	74	125	75	4.05	—	4.07 + 72	.7593
DEC	88	75	150	300	3.55	—	3.54 + 69	.7593
DEC	88	76		1	3.05	2.20	3.08 + 63	.7593
DEC	88	80	200	600	1.04	—	1.69 + 41	.7593

Month	Strike	Vol	Int	High	Low	Sett	PtChg	Future Sett
			S-FRANC PUT					
APR	88	68		55	—	—	CAB	- 1	.7401
APR	88	69	1	327	.01	—	CAB	- 2	.7401
APR	88	70	160	223	.01	—	C1	- 3	.7401
APR	88	71	567	872	.10	.02	.03	- 6	.7401
APR	88	72	929	1422	.32	.06	.08	- 16	.7401
APR	88	73	714	843	.70	.17	.21	- 42	.7401
APR	88	74	208	273	.94	.50	.55	- 77	.7401
APR	88	75		177	—	—	1.21	- 100	.7401
MAY	88	67		17	—	—	.01	- 3	.7401
MAY	88	69	42	45	.15	—	.05	- 7	.7401
MAY	88	70	145	135	.26	—	.11	- 11	.7401
MAY	88	71	84	156	.44	.23	.21	- 20	.7401
MAY	88	72	169	274	.73	.40	.38	- 32	.7401
MAY	88	73	23	154	1.16	.67	.65	- 47	.7401
MAY	88	74	1	1	1.41	1.10	1.08	- 108	.7401
JUN	88	63		209	—	—	.01	- 1	.7401
JUN	88	64		221	.04	—	.02	- 1	.7401
JUN	88	65		261	.03	—	.03	- 1	.7401
JUN	88	66		860	.06	—	.05		.7401
JUN	88	67	1	660	.08	.08	.08	- 1	.7401
JUN	88	68	29	350	.15	11	.12	- 3	.7401
JUN	88	69	59	492	.28	17	.15	- 6	.7401
JUN	88	70	180	1029	.48	.28	.30	- 12	.7401
JUN	88	71	211	543	.73	.43	.46	- 21	.7401
JUN	88	72	116	2554	1.07	.65	.70	- 32	.7401
JUN	88	73	560	1594	1.52	.95	1.03	- 44	.7401
JUN	88	74	585	718	1.80	1.40	1.47	- 57	.7401
JUN	88	75		275	2.30	—	2.04	- 68	.7401
JUN	88	76	4	200	3.09	2.75	2.73	- 75	.7401
JUN	88	77		162	—	—	3.48	- 84	.7401
JUN	88	78		6	—	—	4.30	- 90	.7401
JUN	88	79		125	—	—	5.17	- 110	.7401
JUN	88	80		200	—	—	6.07	- 115	.7401
SEP	88	69	1	175	.72	—	.55	- 18	.7494
SEP	88	70		110	.87	.78	.73	- 22	.7494
SEP	88	71	1	62	1.28	1.00	.96	- 29	.7494
SEP	88	72	4	3	1.63	1.21	1.24	- 35	.7494
SEP	88	73		325	2.08	1.65	1.57	- 43	.7494
SEP	88	74	261	735	2.57	1.96	1.97	- 51	.7494
SEP	88	75		16	2.70	2.50	2.45	- 59	.7494
SEP	88	76		123	3.30	—	3.00	- 68	.7494
SEP	88	77		672	—	—	3.62	- 73	.7494
SEP	88	78		315	—	—	4.29	- 79	.7494
SEP	88	80		150	—	—	5.79	- 90	.7494
DEC	88	70	100	100	1.15	1.08	1.04	- 104	.7593
DEC	88	71		1	1.60	1.27	1.27	- 28	.7593
DEC	88	74	125	75	2.70	2.24	2.25	- 43	.7593
DEC	88	75	150	300	3.20	2.70	2.65	- 50	.7593
TOTAL		VOLUME	OPEN INT					
CALL		7656	21037					
PUT		5430	18595					
COMBINED		13086	39632					

Treasury Bonds

Mth	Strike	Vol	Open Int	High	Week's Low	Last	Net Change	Futures Close
			CALLS					
Jun	88	68	2848	1494	4 00	2 58	1 45	— 31	90 29
Jun	88	90	25745	23707	2 35	1 48	2 23	— 10	90 29
Jun	88	92	46116	36022	1 30	58	1 19	— 08	90 29
Jun	88	94	57324	47222	49	29	43	— 07	90 29
Jun	88	96	39537	33982	26	14	22	— 03	90 29
Jun	88	98	23084	24906	14	07	13	+ 01	90 29
Jun	88	100	12640	21065	07	04	07	— 01	90 29
Jun	88	102	3240	8104	05		04		90 29
Sep	88	92	1161	3127	1 63	1 35	1 56	— 04	89 29
Sep	86	94	1201	10811	1 21	62	1 15	— 03	89 29
Sep	88	96	1830	6141	53	36	52	— 02	89 29
Sep	88	98	2501	3525	34	24	30	— 02	89 29
Sep	88	100	903	1376	22	14	20	— 02	89 29
Dec	98	94	783	934	1 42	1 28	1 38		88 30

Mth	Strike	Vol	Open Int	High	Week's Low	Last	Net Change	Futures Close
			PUTS					
Jun	88	82	6724	8863	18	11	11	— 03	90 29
Jun	88	84	1318	10907	30	18	19	— 02	90 29
Jun	88	86	40009	35020	51	31	31	— 04	90 29
Jun	88	88	57630	37445	1 20	53	56	— 07	90 29
Jun	88	90	71330	40710	2 03	1 23	1 29	— 07	90 29
Jun	88	92	35101	32671	3 11	2 15	2 25	— 03	90 29
Jun	88	94	4258	21033	4 44	3 25	3 50	— 34	90 29
Sep	88	82	3124	2482	1 00	50	50	— 02	89 29
Sep	88	84	1386	3028	1 30	57	1 10	— 03	89 29
Sep	88	86	2260	1805	1 63	1 34	1 38	— 06	89 29
Sep	88	88	942	1088	2 47	2 10	2 10	— 06	89 29
Sep	88	90	3653	3469	3 26	3 60	3 00	— 08	89 29
Sep	88	92	1168	2091	4 44	3 52	4 00	— 10	89 29

Call Volume 221.022: Open Int 245.626
Put Volume 242.142: Open Int 218.290
Volume Friday through Thu.
Open Interest as of close Thu.
High and low Mon. thru Thu., close Fri.
Strikes with less than 500 contracts traded not shown.

option is a very small price to pay for the protection given, considering the potential for profit on the futures contract.

2.   Covered Option Writing

This strategy is initiated by selling an out-of-the-money call (put) option against a long (short) futures position. The best time to initiate this strategy is when a market is at a very over-sold (put) or overbought (call) condition and the trader expects consolidation to occur. The trader receives premium (additional income) from the sale of the option in this situation. Many times the options sold can be profitable even if the market continues to move higher (calls sold), because the decay in their time value outweigh the move in the underlying future contract. It also requires no additional margin other than that already used for the futures position.

3.   Protecting a Futures Position by Combining the Purchase of a Put With a Sale of a Call

This strategy is simply combining the above two strategies and is recommended any time a position is at a substantial profit. This position will allow a trader to have total downside protection, and the potential for additional profit, all at little or no premium cost. This is because the premium for purchasing the puts is paid for by selling the call. (The above three hedging positions are discussed in more detail in Chapter 4.)

4.   Buy a Low-priced Option When a Contract is About to Expire

In the last several weeks prior to expiration, you can purchase options with little time value remaining.

For example, an at-the-money gold option with about two weeks to trade can be purchased for about $200. If your were to predict a gold move correctly, you would make only $200 less than you could have made with a futures contract. But at the same time you have limited your losses to $200 if the market moves against you.

5.   Use Options in Volatile Markets

You may have strong feelings that a market is about to make an explosive move, but the risk involved in taking a net futures position is too great. You can still trade the market in such situations with limited risk by purchasing options or using option spreads.

6.   Use Options to Profit from Trading Range Markets

More than 80% of the time markets are in a trading range. Net traders are often frustrated and frequently stopped out of positions. By using neutral option strategies, a trader can increase his trading opportunities and trade these markets. These kinds of markets, in fact, provide the option strategist opportunities that have some of the highest mathematical probability.

As the market moves up and down, the total position is affected little because as the underlying futures price begins toward an option sold the loss will be compensated by a gain on the option on the other side. Both options lose time value each day. This continual loss of time value on both sides of the trade makes this strategy attractive anytime there is a neutral or non-trending market.

7.   Use Options When You Need Lower Margin Requirements

Reduced margins for many option strategies allow you to develop a diversified portfolio with less capital. Many options strategies require no margin at all. You pay only a premium that is the maximum amount you can lose if the market moves adversely, which is also often less than a futures margin.

8.   Higher Probability of Profit

By proper use of option premiums, positions can be constructed having a higher probability of profit than a futures position. For example, when volatility is high, ratio spreads, constructed by purchasing fairly valued close-to-the-money options and selling overvalued out-of-the-money options, have a very high probability of profit.

9.   Increased Risk/reward Ratio

By taking advantage of disparities in option premium by selling overvalued and/or buying undervalued options, trades can be initiated that have reduced risks, but still have significant profit potential.

10.   Increased Trading Opportunities

There are circumstances in many markets that provide opportunities for the options strategist where it would be inadvisable for an outright position because of lack of trend or too much volatility. Additionally, the option strategist is the only trader that can trade flat, trendless markets profitably.

CHAPTER 7

USING A COMPUTER WHEN TRADING OPTIONS

Many traders have avoided options because of the complexities involved—such as premium evaluations, hedge ratios, betas, deltas, volatility, time value decay, etc. Option traders who do not have a working knowledge of these factors can be at a disadvantage. Computer programmers have attempted to make traders' decisions easier.

The programs developed for both personal computers and large mainframes are similar in several aspects including the fact that they all use pricing models and formulas to determine the theoretical value of options.

Factors used to determine these values also are fairly similar in that the variables considered include the option's strike price, price of the underlying instrument, time left until expiration, interest rates and the calculated volatility of the option. These programs figure theoretical premium values, risk/reward ratios, and hedge and conversion factors.

However, traders who rely on computer-generated figures only are at a disadvantage in trading options. This is because the state of development in computer software in options has not yet progressed enough to be able to factor in all the variables on which an experienced trader would rely.

An option program that properly fits the trader's needs, however, can be a great aid in trade selection and monitoring market strategies. The computer can also be a great time saver in calculating actual volatility, hedge ratios and other data.

Just as there are many computer services available to evaluate options and option strategies, there is also a wide range of other kinds of analysis services available. Some specialize in graphics capability and some scan option premiums for the best to use in certain strategies. Others specialize in arbitrage opportunities and position risk evaluations.

OPTIONS PREMIUM VALUATIONS

What kind of analysis do you need? How much does it cost? Before you can answer these questions, you must examine the basics of premium valuation.

Options premium valuations are calculated from these four variables, three of which are determined easily at any point in time:

1. Number of trading days left until the option expires.

2. Amount the option is in-the-money or out-of-the-money (relationship of the option strike price to the underlying instrument value).

3. Risk-free rate of return (usually the current T-bill or bank rate).

4. Volatility of the option premium (a measure of the swings in the option premium over a period of time).

Option Volatility

Option volatility is the hardest factor to quantify. This last input to the Black-Scholes, Parkinson or other valuation model that an option pricing program uses to evaluate puts and calls causes the greatest headache for option traders.

Volatility measurements are historical, by definition, and are determined by putting the date into the option valuation model "backwards." That is, settlement price, trading days until expiration, risk-free interest rate and in-the-money or out-of-the-money amounts are used to find one missing variable: the volatility.

This calculated volatility from the value the market is placing on the option is known as "floor volatility" or "Market Implied Volatility" (MIV). That changes from day to day and even from moment to moment. Because option valuation services use some form of MIV to calculate theoretical option prices for the present and future, it really depends on what form the MIV enters the model.

Typically, an option valuation service will use a moving average of weighted moving average of MIVs over a period of time. Differences in theoretical valuations result from the weighting (if any) and the period used in the MIV averaging calculation.

Heavier weighting to recent MIVs and a shorter period will result in theoretical pricings that change more quickly and usually will be slower to a day's settlement price. A longer period with no weighting can result in theoretical price consistently too high or too low.

These differences can result in two option programs coming to greatly different theoretical values, which can severely affect the results of an option strategy. The solution to the dilemma is to look at volatility and option premium valuations over a period of time in each market. Daily MIVs are compared with historical data to determine if options in that market can be used with various options strategies effectively. For example, in a period when options are relatively inexpensive historically, you might consider strategies involving buying options. In periods of high volatility, you may want to initiate ratio spreads.

Hedge Ratio

The second important calculation, a by-product of the option valuation model, is the hedge ratio or delta—the amount an option premium will change with a small change in the underlying instrument. A hedge ratio of 0.50 means that if the underlying instrument moves up $1, the option premium will move up 50 cents.

A rule of thumb is that if any underlying instrument is right at the strike price of an option, the option will have a hedge ratio of 0.50. Naturally, hedge ratios change as the in-the-money amount changes, so an option's hedge ratio is always changing.

Hedge ratios must also be considered when formulating option strategies. For example, if you expect the price of gold to increase by $10 an ounce and the hedge ratio of the option you purchase is 0.20, the option will increase by only $2. This may barely cover commissions on the trade. On the other hand, if you write options, you generally want the hedge ratio to be low so that a large fluctuation in the underlying instrument will not severely affect your profit on a position.

Hedge ratios of related options can be combined to provide a spread hedge ratio. In a vertical call bull spread, for example, the hedge ratio of the short call of the higher strike price is subtracted from the hedge ratio of the long call at the lower strike price to provide the spread hedge ratio. This figure will estimate the response of the spread as a whole to change in the underlying futures price. You can determine hedge ratios for other option combinations in the same manner.

A "delta neutral" spread is often used because of its unique characteristics. Delta neutral means that the combined option hedge ratios add up to zero. (Hedge ratios of long puts and short calls are considered negative numbers.) This will make the spread unresponsive to small changes in the underlying futures and is useful for strategies that capitalize on option premium decay.

The underlying futures hedge ratio, of course, is equal to 1 on a long position and -1 on a short position. Delta neutral strategies sometimes may require frequent adjustment, so careful monitoring is important.

Another statistic that a few programs will generate is the responsiveness of option premiums to volatility changes. This calculation can be especially useful for delta neutral strategies to determine at what volatility levels their strategies acquire undesirable characteristics.

Computer data can be obtained either "off-line" or "on-line." Off-line data is data that is obtained through various vendors after market hours. On-line data refers to real time price quotes and analysis as the markets actually trade.

Many traders assume that expensive on-line equipment is necessary. That is not always the case, there are successful traders who only use weekly chart books. On-line option evaluation software is not a guarantee of making profits. In fact, if used improperly or without a good trading plan, it will only increase your losses by the cost of the equipment.

OFF-LINE OPTION ANALYSIS

Over twenty different firms provide various forms of option analysis software. The costs vary from $99 to $1,000+. Although most provide the basic services described above, they differ mainly in the extent of their analysis and their "user friendliness." Any software should be sampled before purchased either through a demo or trial period. Most manufacturers of software provide this for potential users.

There is one program that, in my opinion, stands in a category by itself. *OptionVue IV* (OptionVue Systems, Inc., 175 East Hawthorn Parkway, Ste. 180, Vernon Hills, IL 60061, 708-816-6610), is perhaps the most sophisticated and user friendly of any off-line systems that I have tried. It is a "comprehensive decision support system" for option trading. Its purpose is to assist the trader in selecting the best option strategy in any given situation. It has "what if" capability and will project profit-loss scenarios. It will generate buy and sell signals based on your price forecast and risk level, as well as determine the best strategy to use. It also tracks, and tracks volatility, expirations and margins.

I asked the analysts at OptionVue to provide commentary and studies on several different trade selections that were being considered. The following is their analysis and commentary.

1. Best short strangle, any market.

We used *OptionVue IV's* data base survey function to discover a market whose current implied volatility was high compared to recent historical levels. Wheat was selected by the program because I.V. (implied volatility) was at a historically high level of 23%, also significantly higher than S.V. (statistical volatility) (16%) (Exhibit 7.1). (Note: Exhibits 7.1 through 7.19 can be found at the end of this chapter)

We asked *OptionVue IV* to find the most attractive strangle to sell, based on the idea that wheat would continue to be priced around 287-1/2 and continue to exhibit a volatility of 16% or so. *OptionVue IV* recommended the following strangle: sell 2 Jul310 calls and sell 2 Jul280 puts (Exhibit 7.2).

Looking at this strategy in the matrix (Exhibit 7.3), the program recommended selling the Jul310 calls because the I.V. on these calls was 26.0%, a good deal higher than the I.V. of other calls at that time. However, the sale of two out-of-the-money calls along with 2 near-the-money puts results in a delta imbalance. If delta neutrality is desired, we might consider increasing the number of calls sold to 4. Referring to the illustration, this brings the total position delta down to +7.69, which is near zero.

The next illustration is a profit/loss graph of this 4 x 2 strangle (Exhibit 7.4). This position yields a profit across a wide range of underlying prices. The dark shaded area represents the 1st standard deviation of underlying wheat prices (presuming a 16% volatility), while the lighter shading encompasses the 2nd standard deviation of underlying wheat prices.

2. Best long straddle in Gold.

The historical volatility chart for Gold shows that levels are currently at an extreme low, hence the recommendation by the program to purchase a straddle (Exhibit 7.5). Anticipating a "spike" back to the 20% level or so, sometime during the next couple of months, we asked *OptionVue IV* to recommend the best straddle (or strangle) to purchase (Exhibit 7.6).

It recommended the following: Buy 2 Oct390 calls and buy 2 Oct350 puts (Exhibit 7.7). The next two illustrations show what this position looks like in the matrix, and how it would perform based on a profit/loss graph (Exhibit 7.8). Again, this graph displays the 1st and 2nd standard deviations of probable prices for the underlying using dark and light shading (Exhibit 7.9).

3. Best bullish strategy in U.S. Bonds.

If we project bonds to go up to 102 in the next three months, *OptionVue IV* recommends a simple call purchase (Exhibit 7.10). (As you can see from the illustration, the top three recommendations are call purchases.) Graphing these, you can see that their performances are very similar, especially around the target price of 102, depicted on the graph as a vertical line (Exhibit 7.11).

The historical volatility chart and a snapshot of the matrix are included for reference (Exhibit 7.12).

4. Hedging a short position in Swiss Franc futures, with Swiss Francs currently at 6800 and expecting them to go lower.

The historical volatility chart shows volatilities to be at a high level (Exhibit 7.13). This suggests selling puts as a hedge rather than purchasing calls. Looking at the matrix, you can see that there are several puts available and trading in the June expiration. Which one you pick depends largely on how much room you want to leave the Franc to go down further (Exhibit 7.14). The illustration shows you shorting the 67's. However, the profit/loss graph shows the results of shorting these (solid line) *or* the 68's (dashed line). Obviously, if you short the 67's, you make more money if the Franc falls below 67.5 or so. In the graph, the shaded area encompasses a hypothetical projected trading range between 65 and 68 (Exhibit 7.15).

Although *OptionVue's* price is much higher ($900-$1400) than most other off-line software packages, its capabilities are also greater than any other software I have seen. It is my opinion that if you are going to use computer software, and risk substantial money in trading, that only the best should be considered.

ON-LINE SYSTEMS FOR EVALUATING OPTIONS

The three most powerful on-line systems that I have identified are *OptionVue, Optionomics*, and *FutureSource*. The differences between them have to do with the type of trading you are doing rather than inherent weaknesses or strengths within each system.

OptionVue on-line is exactly the same as we have described for the off-line system above except that instead of manual input, prices, graphs and scenarios are updated real time. This requires an additional $500 package from *OptionVue* along with a monthly fee from a quote vendor of $500+.

Optionomics (3191 South Valley Street, Suite 155, Salt Lake City, UT, 84109, 800-255-3374), provides on-line option evaluation, similar to OptionVue, but in a somewhat more advanced package, with extra "bells & whistles." *Optionomics* sophisticated option evaluations may be lost on the average off-floor trader. We feel that it is better suited for the professional option trader or floor trader who is able to take advantage of its advanced functions. Exhibits 7.16 and 7.17 are examples of information generated from *Optionomics*.

FutureSource (955 Parkview Blvd., Lombard, IL 60148, 800-621-2628), is an on-line system combining futures and options charts and option evaluation. It allows you to use your own computer and access all of these services in one easy to use machine. I find it convenient and time saving, particularly in being able to switch back and forth at a single key stroke from current prices to charts of up to 15 years, and then in being able to switch quickly to evaluation of option strategies. Although missing a few features from specialized option software, its speed, convenience, and reasonable price for on-line data make it a very practical choice. Exhibits 7.18 and 7.19 are *FutureSource's* computer generated trade sheets analyzing the value of the December bond 94 call for market prices between 90 and 100 at three dates I selected in the future.

I keep my uses of a computer very simple in my trading.

1. I calculate option volatility to determine whether it is high or low (I have monthly calculations for at least five years in all options);

2. I calculate the "fair value" of all of the option strike prices and monitor based on the current implied volatility; and

3. I have a "spread sheet" of what my gain or loss will be if the market moves up or down in the future.

4. I have the computer scan for the best strategies in the selected markets.

Remember, your computer can be a valuable aid; but you must still act as the trader and make the final decision on all trades.

Exhibit 7.1
Short Strangle

Exhibit 7.2
Attractive Strangle to Sell

```
              * * *  OPTIONVUE IV SELECTIONS  * * *
------------------------------------------------------------------------
  SYMBOL: WN1         TODAY'S DATE: MAY 08 1991   VALUATION DATE: JUN 15 1991
 CAPITAL: $4,000            PRICE: 287 1/2        CALL VLTY:  21.9 21.9 21.9
STRATEGY: Sell Naked Straddles                     PUT VLTY:  21.9 21.9 21.9
TG.PRICE: Bell curve centered around 287 1/2        INTRST:  7.9%
 RANKING BASIS:  50% Exp.Ret. / 50% 1st St.Dev.Downside Exp.Ret.
------------------------------------------------------------------------
        Recommended Trade                             Exp.Ret.   St.Dev.
        ----------------                              --------   ------
  1.  S   2 Jul310c  @2 1/2,    S   2 Jul280p  @4 5/8   +347      ~521
  2.  S   2 Jul300c  @3 3/4,    S   2 Jul280p  @4 5/8   +339      ~599
  3.  S   3 Sep320c  @5 7/8,    S   3 Sep280p  @5 7/8   +209      ~376
  4.  S   2 Jul290c  @6 3/4,    S   2 Jul290p  @9 3/8   +373      ~849
  5.  S   3 Sep330c  @4 1/8,    S   3 Sep280p  @5 7/8   +215      ~399
  6.  S   2 Jul300c  @3 3/4,    S   2 Jul290p  @9 3/8   +382      ~869
  7.  S   3 Sep310c  @8 5/8,    S   3 Sep280p  @5 7/8   +223      ~461
  8.  S   2 Jul310c  @2 1/2,    S   2 Jul290p  @9 3/8   +389      ~894
  9.  S   2 Jul290c  @6 3/4,    S   2 Jul280p  @4 5/8   +330      ~791
 10.  S   2 Jul320c  @1 1/4,    S   2 Jul280p  @4 5/8   +252      ~529
 11.  S   2 Sep310c  @8 5/8,    S   2 Sep300p  @14 1/4  +155      ~383
 12.  S   2 Jul280c  @11 3/4,   S   2 Jul290p  @9 3/8   +307      ~789


              [ END OF REPORT.  Press any key... ]
```

Exhibit 7.3
Strangle to Sell Matrix

```
OPTIONVUE IV            MATRIX         Wheat (CBT)*          WED MAY 8 1991
/FUTURES===================================================================\
| |=======JUL=(54)========| |-------SEP-(118)-------| |-------DEC-(208)-------||
|  287 1/2        11:13   296 3/4 296 3/4   11:13   309 1/2 309 1/2   11:13 |
|OPTIONS===================================================================|
|!        |-----JUL-(38)-------| |-----SEP-(101)------| |-----DEC-(192)-----||
|CALLS   2 1/2   15.0    -4    8 3/4   36.6  _____   18      50.6   _____   |
|310     26.0%  WYN31  2 1/2   22.9%  WYU31  _____   19.1%  WYZ31   _____   |
|CALLS   3 3/4   28.3   _____   12 1/2   47.5  _____   23 1/4  58.4   _____   |
|300     22.8%  WYN30   _____   21.2%  WYU30  _____   21.6%  WYZ30   _____   |
|CALLS>  6 3/4   46.1   _____   17 1/2   58.9  _____   29 1/2  66.0   _____   |
|290     21.5%  WYN29   _____   21.4%  WYU29  _____   21.9%  WYZ29   _____   |
|^       -----------------------------------------------------------------  |
|PUTS    15 1/2  -70.9  _____   14 1/2  -50.4  _____   13 3/4  -37.6   _____   |
|300     20.7%  WZN30   _____   20.9%  WZU30  _____   21.3%  WZZ30   _____   |
|PUTS>   9 1/2   -53.0  _____   9 1/4   -39.0  _____   10     -30.0   _____   |
|290     22.2%  WZN29   _____   20.4%  WZU29  _____   20.7%  WZZ29   _____   |
|PUTS    4 1/2   -33.8   -2    6      -28.1  _____   6 1/2   -22.9   _____   |
|280     21.5%  WZN28  4 5/8   21.2%  WZU28  _____   20.8%  WZZ28   _____   |
|                                                                          |
|SUMMARY===================================================================|
| Orig.Reqmt:    $2,025  Commis:  $150.00   Delta:  +7.69   AvgMIV: 21.8% |
|Maint.Reqmt:    $3,444                     Gamma:  -8.16   Calls: 22.1% |
| Cash Flow:     +$812   Theta:  +$22.07/day  Vega:  -78.2    Puts: 21.2% |
\- [F1]=Help -------------------------------------------------------- 22K ----/
```

Exhibit 7.4
Profit/Loss of Strangle to Sell

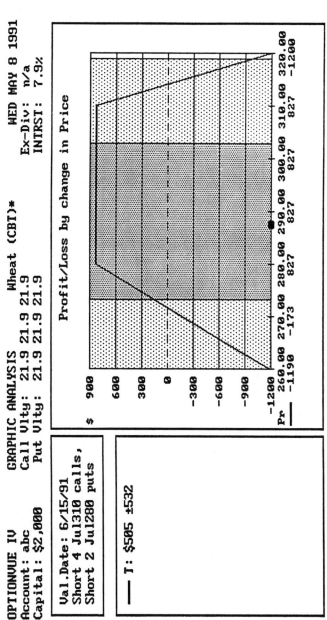

OPTIONVUE IV   GRAPHIC ANALYSIS   Wheat (CBT)*   WED MAY 8 1991
Account: abc   Call Vlty: 21.9 21.9 21.9   Ex-Div: n/a
Capital: $2,000   Put Vlty: 21.9 21.9 21.9   INTRST: 7.9%

Val.Date: 6/15/91
Short 4 Jul310 calls,
Short 2 Jul280 puts

—— T: $505 ±532

Profit/Loss by change in Price

```
 $ 900

   600

   300

     0

  -300

  -600

  -900

 -1200
Pr  260.00 270.00 280.00 290.00 300.00 310.00 320.00
    -1190   -173    827    827    827    827   -1200
```

Exhibit 7.5
Long Straddle

Gold (CEC) Volatilities

20-Day Statistical   ---- Implied

OPTIONVUE IV

Exhibit 7.6
Straddle to Purchase

```
OPTIONVUE IV        DEF. SELECTION        Gold (CEC)*          WED MAY 8 1991
-----------------------------------------------------------------------------

                    Valuation Date: JUL 13 1991
                      Target Type: [Bell]/Price/Range
                     Center Price: 358.70
                       Volatility:  20.0%
                         Strategy: [Purchase straddles]/...
                 Capital Provided: $2,500
                 Comparison Basis: [P/L]/Yield/Ann.Yield
                Volatility Change: +5.0%
                Int.Rate Change: 0.00%

                          RANKING BASIS
                    Proportion Exp.Ret:  1
              Proportion Downside Exp.Ret:  1




-- [F1]=Help ------------------------------------------------------ 77K -----
```

Exhibit 7.7
Long Straddle Recommendations

```
                    * * *  OPTIONVUE IV SELECTIONS  * * *
-----------------------------------------------------------------------------
    SYMBOL: GCM1        TODAY'S DATE: MAY 08 1991      VALUATION DATE: JUL 13 1991
   CAPITAL: $2,500             PRICE: 358.70           CALL VLTY:  19.7 19.7 19.7
  STRATEGY: Buy Straddles                               PUT VLTY:  19.7 19.7 19.7
  TG.PRICE: Bell curve centered around 358.70            INTRST:   7.9%
  RANKING BASIS:  50% Exp.Ret. / 50% 1st St.Dev.Downside Exp.Ret.
-----------------------------------------------------------------------------
       Recommended Trade                                Exp.Ret.    St.Dev.
       ------------------                                --------    -------
  1.  B   2 Oct390c @4.50,    B   2 Oct350p @6.40        +1,141      ~1,865
  2.  B   2 Oct380c @6.70,    B   2 Oct340p @4.00        +1,150      ~2,060
  3.  B   2 Oct390c @4.50,    B   2 Oct340p @4.00         +985       ~1,756
  4.  B   1 Oct370c @9.60,    B   1 Oct360p @10.30        +773       ~1,088
  5.  B   1 Oct360c @14.20,   B   1 Oct360p @10.30        +780       ~1,182
  6.  B   1 Oct370c @9.60,    B   1 Oct350p @6.40         +758       ~1,137
  7.  B   1 Oct360c @14.20,   B   1 Oct360p @10.30        +765       ~1,300
  8.  B   1 Oct380c @6.70,    B   1 Oct360p @10.30        +684       ~1,041
  9.  B   1 Oct380c @6.70,    B   1 Oct350p @6.40         +669       ~1,010
 10.  B   1 Oct370c @9.60,    B   1 Oct340p @4.00         +678       ~1,221
 11.  B   1 Oct360c @14.20,   B   1 Oct340p @4.00         +685       ~1,434
 12.  B   1 Oct390c @4.50,    B   1 Oct360p @10.30        +601       ~1,044

                    [ END OF REPORT.  Press any key... ]
```

Exhibit 7.8
Long Straddle Performance Based on Profit/Loss

```
OPTIONVUE IV        MATRIX        Gold (CEC) *              WED MAY 8 1991
```

FUTURES	JUN=(26) 358.70 11:39	AUG-(85) 361.30 361.60 11:39	OCT-(146) 364.70 364.50 11:39

OPTIONS	JUN-(3)	AUG-(66)	OCT-(129)	
v				
CALLS 390	.... 0.00 OGM390	1.40 11.4 OGQ390 15.3%	4.40 22.7 OGV390 15.2%	+2 4.50
CALLS 380	0.10 0.00 OGM380	2.50 21.5 OGQ380 14.3%	6.60 32.5 OGV380 14.8%	
CALLS 370	0.10 0.99 OGM370	4.80 35.8 OGQ370 13.8%	9.50 43.9 OGV370 14.1%	
!				
PUTS 370	11.50 -98.9 OGI370	14.10 -62.8 OGO370 15.0%	15.70 -53.4 OGR370 15.3%	
PUTS> 360	2.50 -60.4 OGI360 13.7%	7.50 -45.8 OGO360 13.5%	10.20 -41.2 OGR360 14.7%	
PUTS 350	0.20 -3.17 OGI350 13.8%	3.80 -29.0 OGO350 13.8%	6.30 -29.5 OGR350 14.7%	+2 6.40

SUMMARY				
Orig.Reqmt: $2,280	Commis: $100.00	Delta: -13.46	AvgMIV: 14.2%	
Maint.Reqmt: $2,280		Gamma: +4.02	Calls: 14.3%	
Cash Flow: -$2,280	Theta: -$15.33/day	Vega: +281	Puts: 13.9%	
[F1]=Help				22K

Exhibit 7.9
1st and 2nd Standard Deviations of Probable Prices

OPTIONVUE IV   GRAPHIC ANALYSIS   Gold (CEC)*   WED MAY 8 1991
Account: abc   Call Vlty: 19.9 19.9 18.7   Ex-Div: n/a
Capital: $2,500   Put Vlty: 19.7 19.7 18.8   INTRST: 7.9%

Val.Date: 7/13/91
Long 2 Oct390 calls,
Long 2 Oct350 puts

Profit/Loss by change in Price

$ 12.0K

10.0K

8.0K

6.0K

4.0K

2.0K

0.0K

-2.0K

Pr 300.00 320.00 340.00 360.00 380.00 400.00 420.00
   6800   3160   442   -498   402   2820   6120

 T: $1272 ±1990

Exhibit 7.10
Call Purchase (U.S. Treasury Bonds)

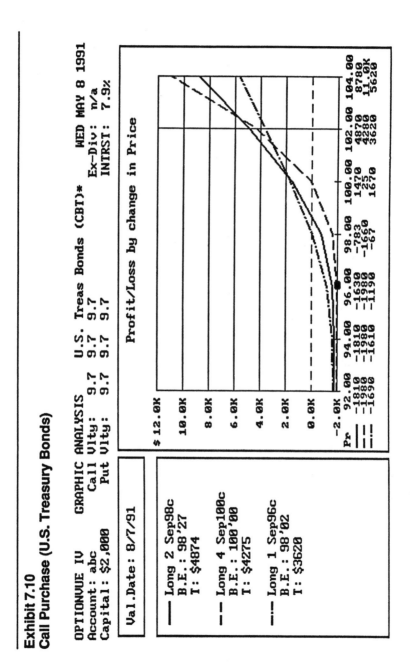

OPTIONVUE IV   GRAPHIC ANALYSIS   U.S. Treas Bonds (CBT)*   WED MAY 8 1991
Account: abc   Call Vlty: 9.7   9.7   9.7   Ex-Div: n/a
Capital: $2,000   Put Vlty: 9.7   9.7   9.7   INTRST: 7.9%

Val.Date: 8/7/91

Profit/Loss by change in Price

$ 12.0K

10.0K

8.0K

6.0K

4.0K

2.0K

0.0K

-2.0K

Pr	92.00	94.00	96.00	98.00	100.00	102.00	104.00
—	-1810	-1810	-1630	-783	1470	4870	8780
--	-1980	-1980	-1980	-1660	25	4280	11.0K
-·-	-1690	-1610	-1190	-67	1670	3620	5620

— Long 2 Sep98c
   B.E.: 98'27
   I: $4874

-- Long 4 Sep100c
   B.E.: 100'00
   I: $4275

-·- Long 1 Sep96c
   B.E.: 98'02
   I: $3620

Exhibit 7.11
Call Purchase (U.S. Treasury)

```
OPTIONVUE IV        MATRIX        U.S. Treas Bonds (CBT)*           WED MAY 8 1991
/FUTURES=====================================================================
|=====JUN=(26)=====| |-----SEP-(118)-----| |-----DEC-(208)-----|
   96'02      14:26    95'09  95'13  14:26    94'20  94'26  14:26
/OPTIONS=====================================================================
|-----JUN-(10)-----| |-----SEP-(108)-----| |-----DEC-(192)-----|
100c   ..:..           0'27    9.2%          1'17    9.6%
 98c   0'07  10.6%      0'55    9.3%          1'56    9.4%
 96c>  0'39   9.1%      1'39    9.6%          2'48    9.3%
 94c   2'11  11.7%      2'45   10.0%          4'00    9.7%
 92c   4'02             4'00   10.0%          4'50    6.2%
 90c   6'02             5'37    9.7%

100p   ..:..           ..:..                 ..:..
 98p   1'62            3'34    9.3%          4'34    9.7%
 96p>  0'36   9.4%      2'18    9.4%          3'17    9.7%
 94p   0'06  10.8%      1'26    9.8%          ..:..
 92p   ..:..           0'50   10.0%          ..:..
 90p   ..:..           0'28   10.5%          ..:..
       Last   MIV  Trade
SUMMARY=====================================================================
 Orig.Reqmt:   $0   Commis:  $0.00     Delta:  0.00    AvgMIV:  9.9%
 Maint.Reqmt:  $0   Theta: $0.00/day   Gamma:  0.00    Calls:   9.9%
 Cash Flow:    $0                      Vega:   0.00    Puts:    9.9%
-[F1]=Help -------------------------------------------------- 22K -----
```

Exhibit 7.12
Historical Volatility Chart (U.S. Treasury Bonds)

U.S. Treas Bonds (CBT) Volatilities.

Oct 13 89 — Jan 16 90 — Apr 20 90 — Jul 24 90 — Oct 26 90 — Jan 29 91 — May 3 91

——— 20-Day Statistical   --- Implied   ——— OPTIONVUE IV

Exhibit 7.13
Historical Volatility Chart (Swiss Franc)

Swiss Franc (IMM) Volatilities

—— 20-Day Statistical   ——— Implied

OPTIONVUE IV

Exhibit 7.14
Profit/Loss Matrix

```
OPTIONVUE IV         MATRIX         Swiss Franc (IMM)*            WED MAY 8 1991
/FUTURES=====JUN==(42)==========|  |------SEP-(133)------|  |------DEC-(224)------|
|   68.17      -2    14:20         67.78       14:20        67.53       14:20
|OPTIONS===========================================================================
|v     |------JUN-(31)------|  |------JUL-(59)------|  |------AUG-(94)------|
|CALLS      .....  CFM685      .....  CFN685      .....  CFQ685
|68.50  13.9%
|CALLS>     .....  CFM680      .....  CFN680      .....  CFQ680
|68.00
|CALLS      .....  CFM675      .....  CFN675      .....  CFQ675
|67.50
|-!
|PUTS>   0.97  1.00  PFM680    .....  PFN680      .....  PFQ680
|68.00  13.6%
|PUTS    0.78  0.82  PFM675    .....  PFN675      .....  PFQ675
|67.50  14.1%
|PUTS    0.57  0.61  PFM670   -2  0.57  PFN670    .....  PFQ670
|67.00  13.8%          13.4%
|SUMMARY============================================================================
| Orig.Reqmt:   $4,600    Commis:   $50.00      Delta: -135.1   AvgMIV: 13.9%
| Maint.Reqmt:  $11,008                         Gamma:  -26.0   Calls:  13.9%
| Cash Flow:   +$1,375    Theta: +$39.79/day    Vega:    -179   Puts:   13.7%
|- [F1]=Help                                                             22K
```

Exhibit 7.15
Projected Trading Range

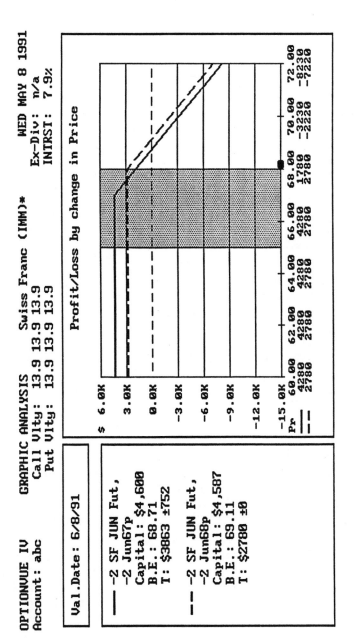

OPTIONVUE IV   GRAPHIC ANALYSIS   Swiss Franc (IMM)*   WED MAY 8 1991
Account: abc   Call Vlty: 13.9 13.9 13.9   Ex-Div: n/a
    Put Vlty: 13.9 13.9 13.9   INTRST: 7.9%

Val.Date: 6/8/91

Profit/Loss by change in Price

—2 SF JUN Fut,
—2 Jun67p
Capital: $4,600
B.E.: 68.71
T: $3863 ±752

-- —2 SF JUN Fut,
-- —2 Jun68p
Capital: $4,587
B.E.: 69.11
T: $2780 ±0

Exhibit 7.16
"Optionomics" On-Line Option Evaluation

```
            LCM1    PREM VAL. 06/07/91        MP   76.13 AIV  10.50 DAYS  43
    82 1.C          86    -28880             82C    .03  11.16    2.7
       2.P          84    -20880              P    5.88   9.58   98.8
    ---------------------  82    -12880       80C    .10  10.29    8.3
    80 3.C          80     -4880 ALPHA=  1.10  P    3.93   9.16   94.1
       4.P          78     3120 UPS  78.33    78C    .35   9.71   23.8
    ---------------------  76     3120 DWS  73.95   P    2.20   9.46   76.8
    78 5.C -  10  .35  74     3120            76C   1.15  10.40   52.6
       6.P          72     -4880              P    1.03  10.50   47.4
    ---------------------  70    -12880        74C   2.53  11.37   77.2
    76 7.C          68    -20880              P     .43  11.75   23.5
       8.P          66    -28880             72C   4.30  13.06   89.7
    ---------------------  NET UPSIDE=   -10   P     .23  14.28   12.2
    74 9.C          NET DNSIDE=    10        70C   6.18  13.66   96.5
      10.P -  10  .43  BASIS SPREAD =    .00   P     .10  15.68    5.6
    ---------------------       To be delta   F3. CHG FUTURES PRICE:
    72 11.C                     neutral       F4. +/- VOLATILITY:
       12.P                YOU NEED TO:  F5. CHG DAYS TO EXP:
    ---------------------          BUY      .03    NET PREM. =       3120.0
    70 13.C              $DELTA=      -12   -.0   TOT COMM =            0
       14.P             $GAMMA=     -892  -2.2   CASH P/L =          .00
    ---------------------     $VEGA =     -644  -1.6   FUTRS P/L=          .00
    LF/SF               $THETA=      572   1.4   EQUITY   =           .0
    LC/SC               Theta Days =  7          ACC VALUE=           .0
    F1=Opt Val IV=Chg IV & GVT F6=%ChgMkt F8=SIMULATE F9=GRAPHS F10=UPDT    OK


                    ***** TODAY'S DATE = 04/25/91 *****
    LCM1  MKT PRICE =  76.13 DAYS TO EXP =  43 AIV =  10.50

        INTRINSIC VALUE               ALPHA=  1.10   NET PREM. =    3120.0
            86     -28880             UPS   78.33
            84     -20880             DWS   73.95
            82     -12880
            80      -4880
            78      3120
            76      3120
            74      3120
            72      -4880
            70     -12880
            68     -20880
            66     -28880             AVE OF TOTAL =    -11425.4545
    --------------------------------------------------------------------
    UPS ALPHA PRICE =  78.33  NET UPS =   -10 BK EVEN UPS =   78.78
                   ALPHA UPS BK EVEN DIF =   .45
                   ALPHA DWS BK EVEN DIF =   .73
    DWS ALPHA PRICE =  73.95  NET DWS =   10 BK  EVEN DWS =  73.22
       MARGIN =     5600 AVE. PROFIT =    3120.0000 SCORE = 470.85%
    --------------------------------------------------------------------

               PRESS ANY KEY TO RETURN TO DISPLAY PAGE
```

Exhibit 7.17
"Optionomics" On-Line Option Evaluation

```
          Opt Price USM2    +/-      %    % of Mkt Chg      MP 107.00 AIV    9.20 DAYS 296
118 Call       .01     .34    34.00    .04    C*          118C    .35        9.20 *   12.7
118 Put      24.39  -13.04    -.53   -.96    P*             P   11.35        9.20 **  87.3
116 Call       .03     .49    16.33    .06               116C    .52        9.20 *   17.5
                                                            P    9.52        9.20 *   82.5
116 Put      22.40  -12.52    -.57   -.94               114C   1.11        9.20 *   23.5
                                                            P    8.11        9.20 *   76.5
114 Call       .04    1.07    17.75    .08               112C   1.42        9.20 *   30.5
                                                            P    6.42        9.20 **  69.5
114 Put      20.42  -12.31    -.60   -.92               110C   2.18        9.20 *   38.5
                                                            P    5.18        9.20 *   61.5
112 Call       .06    1.36    16.67    .11      F3. CHG FUTURES PRICE:
                                               F4. +/- VOLATILITY:
112 Put      18.44  -12.02    -.64   -.89      F5. CHG DAYS TO EXP:
                                               F6. CHG COMM RATE :
110 Call       .10    2.08    13.60    .16
                                               SET FOR BUYING OF OPTIONS
110 Put      16.48  -11.30    -.68   -.84      C / P       COST      +/-      %
                                               118/ 110  16.49-10.60        -.65
Orig. Mkt Price  =   93.13  Mkt Chg  = 13.19   116/ 112  18.47-11.17        -.60
Orig. Volatility =    9.20  VOLAT CHG =   .00   114/ 114  20.46-11.24        -.55
Orig. Days to Exp=     386  DAYS CHG  =  -90    114/ 112  18.48-10.59        -.58
F1=OPT VALUE,F2=SET TRADES,F8=CHG MKT PRC %,   116/ 110  16.51-10.45        -.64
F10= HELP                                           OK
```

Exhibit 7.18
"FutureSource" Trade Sheet

Option:	US	Valuation Date: 7/27/90	Interest: 8.07	Div/For: 0.00

Futures	Theoretical Market Value			Futures Prices				
	Time: 8/01/90	9/15/90	11/15/90	Sim	U	MY	Spread	Value
9000	30	15	0		Y	U0		9325
9020	39	21	0	*	Y	Z0	-9	9316
9100	50	29	0		Y	H1	-12	9304
9128	62	39	2		Y	M1	-6	9238
9216	112	52	5		Y	U1	-11	9219
9304	128	103	12		Y	Z1	-8	9211
9324	147	121	26		Y	H2		
9412	203	141	47		Y	M2		
9500	226	281	111					
9520	251	227	144	Range: FUTURES				
9600	314	255	218	From:	9000			
9628	342	321	256	To:	10000			
9716	409	354	332					
9804	440	424	400	Contour: TIME				
9824	510	459	448	- - - :	8/01/90			
9912	544	532	524	- - - :	9/15/90			
10000	615	606	600	——— :	11/15/90			

Exhibit 7.19
"FutureSource" Trade Sheet

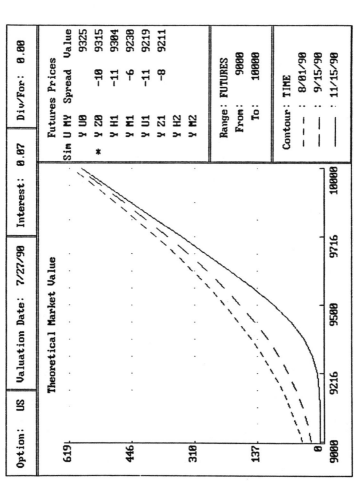

| Option: | US | Valuation Date: | 7/27/90 | Interest: | 0.07 | Div/For: | 0.00 |

Theoretical Market Value

Futures Prices

Sim	U MY	Spread	Value
	Y U0		9325
*	Y Z0	-10	9315
	Y H1	-11	9304
	Y M1	-6	9230
	Y U1	-11	9219
	Y Z1	-8	9211
	Y H2		
	Y M2		

Range: FUTURES
From: 9000
To: 10000

Contour: TIME
- - - : 8/01/90
— — : 9/15/90
——— : 11/15/90

APPENDIX

VOLATILITY CHARTS 1988-1990

The following are charts of implied volatility from 1988 through 1990 of some of the most popular markets. (These charts are courtesy of Optionomics, 3191 South Valley Street, Ste 155, Salt Lake City, Utah, 84109, 800-255-3374.)

The first three charts are of the S&P 500. They show volatility starting at a relatively high point in the 30% range in early 1988. The market was just coming off the October crash and volatility, although receding from the extremely high levels in October, was still relatively high. It then continued to decline into November. As mentioned in Chapter 3, low volatility often is a predecessor to major market moves. In fact, the S&P began its rise at that time from the 260 level, rising to over 360 in less than one year. Extreme increases in volatility can be seen in October of 1989 when the mini-decline occurred, and again in August through October of 1990 when the market dropped to the 300 range.

Charts 4, 5 and 6 represent treasury bond volatility. 1988 was a particularly good year to sell bond options, because as the market remained in a trading range, volatility of the options declined from 16% at the beginning of the year to 10% at the end of the year. This decline of volatility caused most options to lose much of their value, making neutral option positions very attractive. You will notice in Chart 6 that the bond's two large moves up in 1990, approximately six points earlier in the year and over ten points at the end of the year, were both preceded by low volatility readings.

Chart 7, 8 and 9 represent crude oil volatility. As can be seen from Chart 9, crude oil volatility increased fivefold during the year, as the crisis in the Gulf unfolded.

Charts 10, 11, and 12 are soybean implied volatility and Charts 13, 14, and 15 represent the corn option market. Of particular note in all six of these charts is the dramatic increase in volatility every year during the summer months. Does this suggest anything to us by the way of option strategies?

Charts 16, 17, and 18 are of gold option volatility and Charts 19, 20, and 21 are of the silver option market. Of particular interest is Chart 20 showing silver making a new low in volatility in early June 1988 which immediately preceded its jump to $8. Charts 22, 23, and 24 are the Japanese Yen options and Charts 25, 26, and 27 Swiss Franc options. Both of these markets declined in volatility throughout 1988 and early 1989, and after making a new low in volatility in early 1989, these markets then commenced huge rallies, increasing over 30% in price.

Finally, Charts 28, 29 and 30 are the live cattle option market. As seen in these charts, volatility typically ranges from 8 to 17%. Live cattle options seem to trade quite differently than other markets, and, during the same time period, different months or strike prices can have volatilities on both ends of the scale. This can be an excellent market for initiating "delta neutral" trades.

These charts can give you an idea of the approximate ranges in volatility that these markets have had in the past. You can then determine whether current implied volatility is relatively high, low, or mediocre. This is, of course, important in determining the best strategy to use when initiating a position in that market.

Chart 1

Chart 2

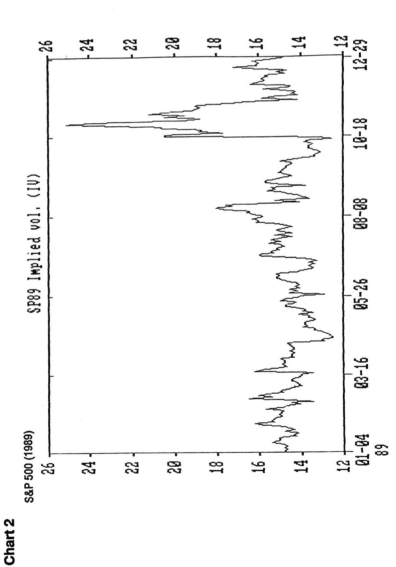

S&P 500 (1989)

SP89 Implied vol. (IV)

Chart 3

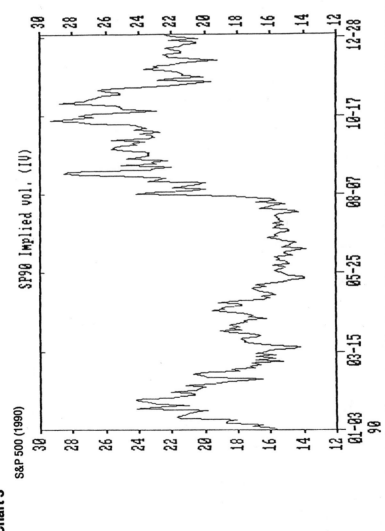

S&P 500 (1990)

SP90 Implied vol. (IV)

Chart 4

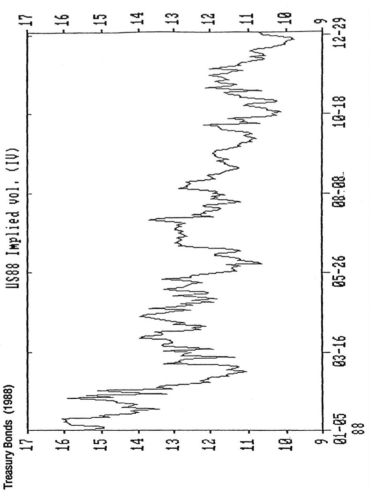

Treasury Bonds (1988)　　　US88 Implied vol. (IV)

Chart 5

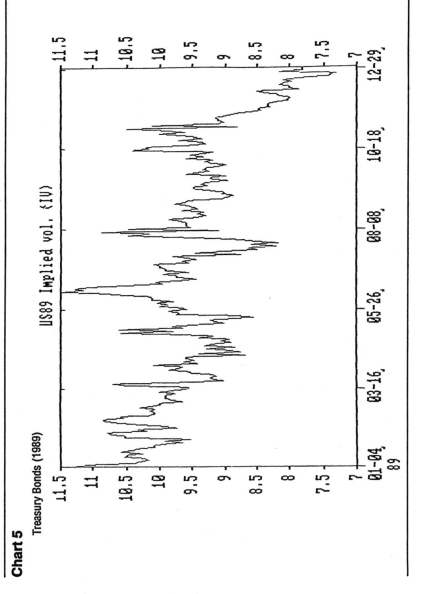

Treasury Bonds (1989)

Chart 6

Treasury Bonds (1990)

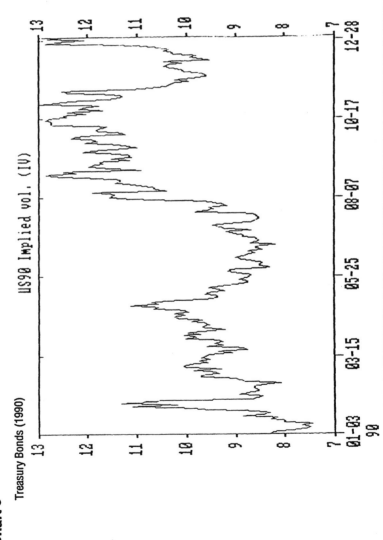

US90 Implied Vol. (IV)

Chart 7

Chart 8

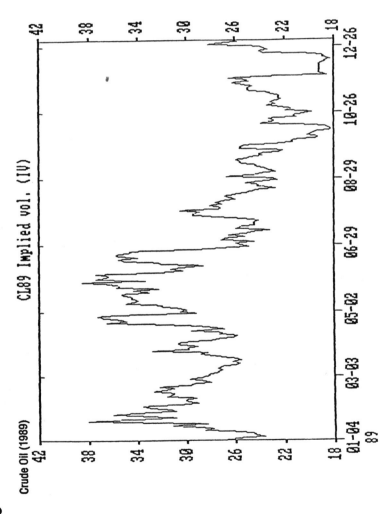

Crude Oil (1989) CL89 Implied vol. (IV)

Chart 9

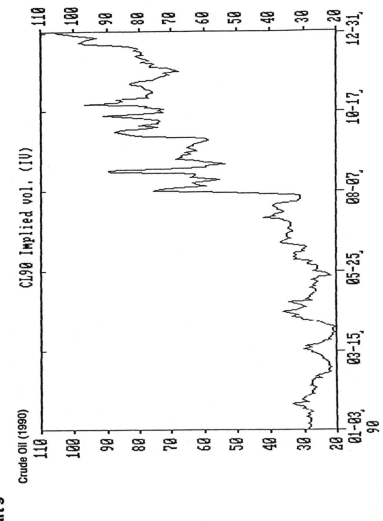

Crude Oil (1990)   CL90 Implied vol. (IV)

Chart 10

Soybeans (1988) $_88 Implied vol. (IV)

Chart 11

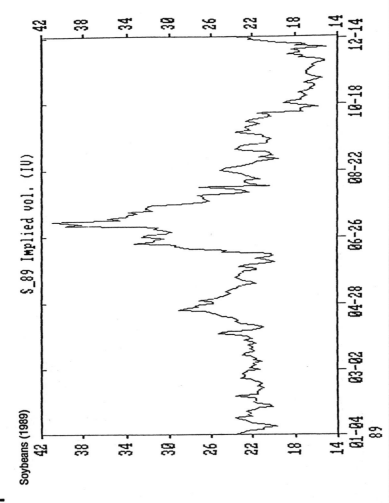

S_89 Implied vol. (IV)

Soybeans (1989)

Chart 12

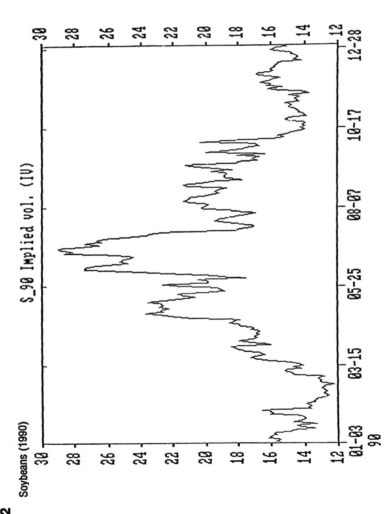

Soybeans (1990)

S_90 Implied vol. (IV)

Chart 13

Chart 14

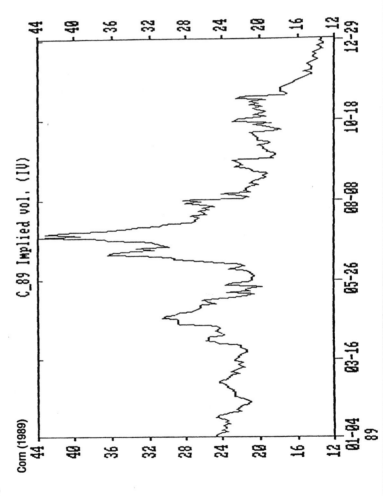

Corn (1989)

C_89 Implied vol. (IV)

Chart 15

Chart 16

Chart 17

Chart 18

Chart 19

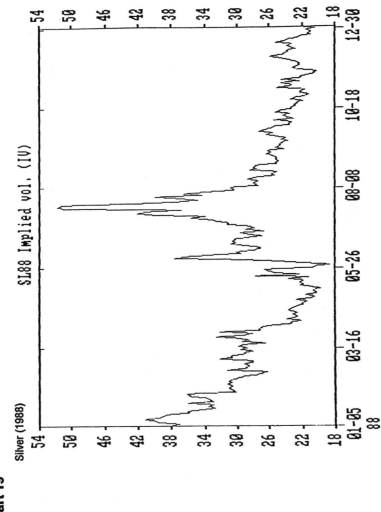

Silver (1988)

SL88 Implied vol. (IV)

Chart 20

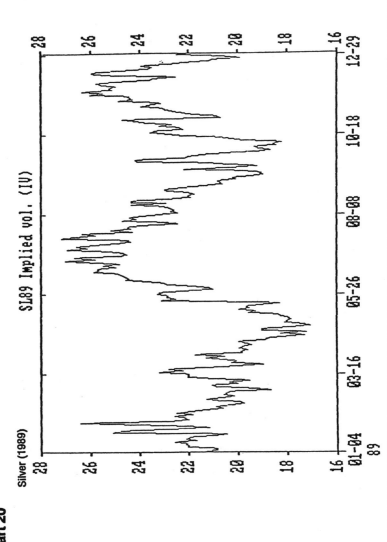

Silver (1989)

SL89 Implied vol. (IV)

Chart 21

Silver (1990)

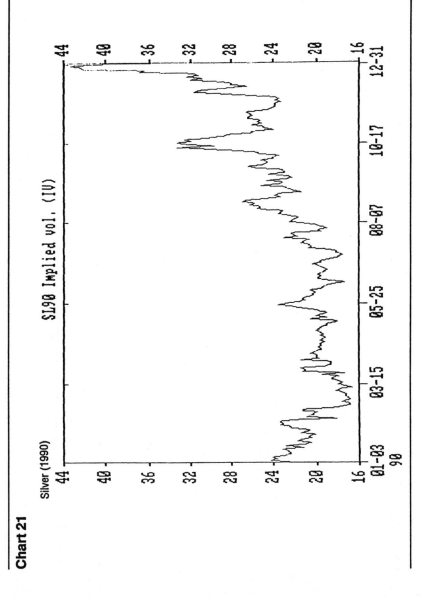

SL90 Implied vol. (IV)

Chart 22

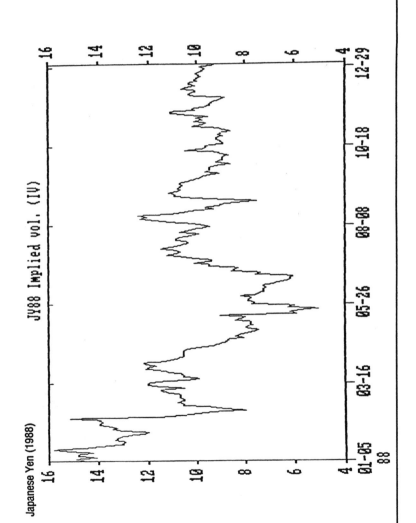

Japanese Yen (1988)

JY88 Implied vol. (IV)

Chart 23

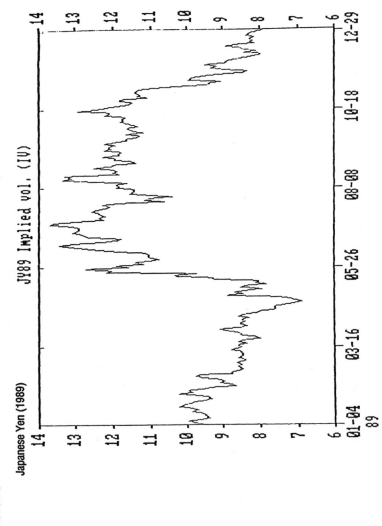

Japanese Yen (1989)   JY89 Implied vol. (IV)

Chart 24

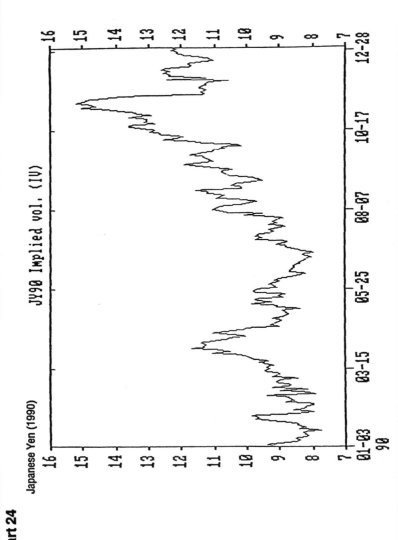

Chart 25

Swiss Franc (1988)

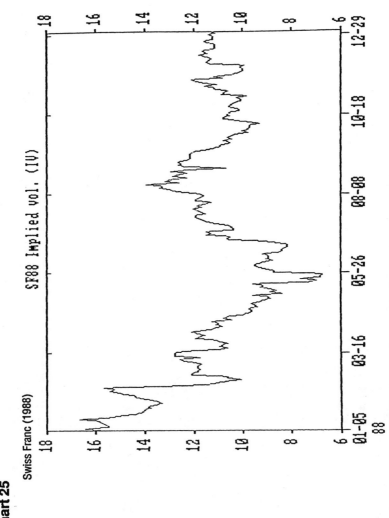

$F88 Implied vol. (IV)

Chart 26

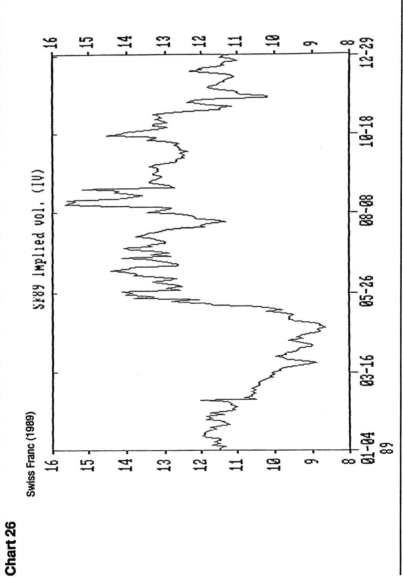

Swiss Franc (1989)

SF89 Implied Vol. (IV)

Chart 27

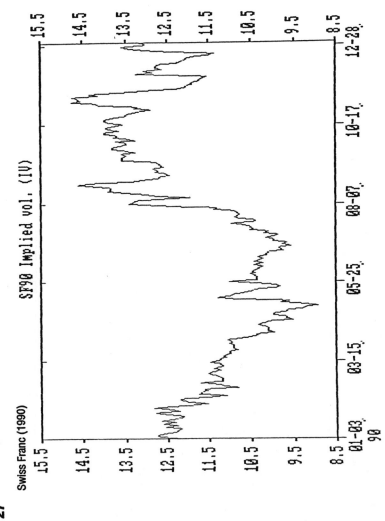

Swiss Franc (1990)   SF90 Implied vol. (IV)

Chart 28

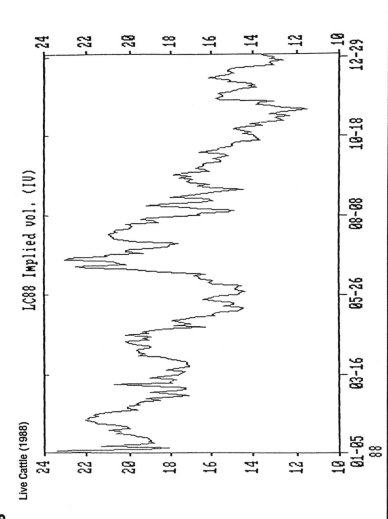

Live Cattle (1988)

LC88 Implied vol. (IV)

Chart 29

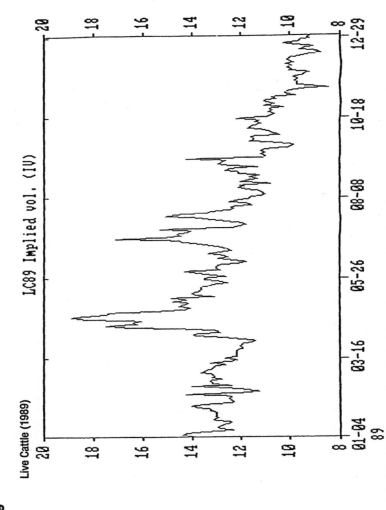

Live Cattle (1989)

LC89 Implied vol. (IV)

Chart 30

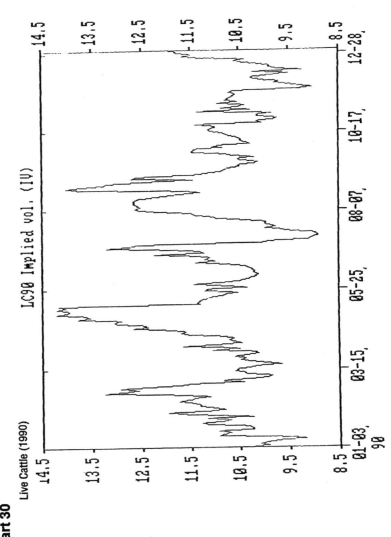

Live Cattle (1990)

LC90 Implied vol. (IV)

GLOSSARY

Arbitrage The simultaneous buying and selling of the same, or equivalent, option in different markets.

Assignment A notice to an option writer that the option has been exercised by the option holder.

At the Money An option whose strike price is equal to the market value of the underlying futures contract.

Beta Measure of how the options market correlates to the movement of the underlying futures market.

Call Option An option which gives the option buyer the right to buy the underlying contract at a specified price within a certain time; and the the seller's obligation to sell the contract for the premium received before the expiration time of the option.

Covered Option An option written against an opposite in the futures or cash market.

Credit Money received from the sale of options.

Debit Money paid for the purchase of options.

Delta The amount by which an options price will change for a unit change in the underlying future's price.

Exercising Options Over 98% of option positions are closed out prior to the expiration of the option period. This is accomplished by the reverse of the initial transaction. For example, an option buyer will sell his position at the current market price for a profit or loss to close out his position; and the option seller will buy back his position to do the same.

However, the option buyer has an additional right to "exercise" his option prior to the expiration. In doing this, the buyer of a call option would give notice to his broker to turn the option into a long futures position; and the purchaser of a put would do the same to turn his option into a short futures contract.

Expiration   Every option must have a specific time during which the option can be traded or exercised. After that time, the option is deemed to have expired and has no value.

Free Trade   An option spread initiated by purchasing a close-to-the-money put or call and later completed by selling a further out-of-the-money put or call of the same expiration period at the same premium. When completed, it requires no margin or capital and has no loss potential.

Hedge   The buying and/or selling of offsetting positions in order to provide protection against an adverse change in price of the contract.

In-the-Money   A term describing any option whose strike price is lower than the future's price for calls and higher than the future's price for puts.

Intrinsic Value   The amount of money that could be realized if the option were to be exercised immediately (out-of-the-money options have no intrinsic value).

Margin   The sum of money which must be deposited and maintained by the seller of option positions.

Naked Writing   Writing an option on a futures contract on which the writer has no cash or futures position.

Neutral Option Position   An option spread initiated by selling an out-of-the-money put and call of the same expiration period to collect premium in a flat or choppy market.

Option   An option is a contract between two parties to purchase or sell a commodity futures contract at a predetermined price within a specific time period. Every option transaction has an option buyer and an option seller.

Option Buyer   A buyer of a put or call option always has the right (not obligation) to purchase (call) or sell (put) the commodities futures contract. For this right he pays a premium, which is the most he can lose even if the market goes drastically against his predicted direction. However, if the market goes in his favor his potential profits are unlimited.

Option Seller   The option seller receives a premium from the option buyer at the time of the option transaction. The option seller has the obligation to sell to the option buyer (call) or purchase for the option buyer (put) a commodities futures contract. For undertaking this obligation, the option seller receives a premium at the time of the opening of the option transaction. This premium is his to keep if the option is not exercised or sold. This option premium is the maximum amount of profit that the option seller can make, and the option seller always has unlimited risk if the market moves against his position.

Out-of-the-Money   An option which has no intrinsic value—a call option whose strike price is higher than the market and a put option whose strike price is lower than the market.

Premium   The premium is the amount of money paid by the option buyer to the option seller to open an option transaction. The option premium represents the maximum amount of money that the option buyer has at risk, while the option seller's maximum profit is restricted to the amount of this option premium.

The amount of premium is determined on the exchange trading floors by negotiation between option buyers and sellers depending on market conditions.

Put Option   An option which gives the buyer the right to sell the futures contract and the seller the obligation to deliver the futures contract at the strike price on or before the expiration date.

Spread   A position consisting of two or more options.

Strike Price   The strike price is the set amount at which a buyer of a call can purchase the underlying futures contract or at which the buyer of a put can sell his contract. Every option transaction must contain this specified price.

Theoretical Value   The price of an option as computed by a mathematical model.

Time Value   The amount by which an option premium exceeds the option's intrinsic value.

Volatility   A measure of the change of an option's premium over a period of time.

INDEX

About the Publisher

PROBUS PUBLISHING COMPANY

Probus Publishing Company fills the informational needs of today's business professional by publishing authoritative, quality books on timely and relevant topics, including:

- Investing
- Futures/Options Trading
- Banking
- Finance
- Marketing and Sales
- Manufacturing and Project Management
- Personal Finance, Real Estate, Insurance and Estate Planning
- Entrepreneurship
- Management

Probus books are available at quantity discounts when purchased for business, educational or sales promotional use. For more information, please call the Director, Corporate/Institutional Sales at 1-800-PROBUS-1, or write:

Director, Corporate/Institutional Sales
Probus Publishing Company
1925 N. Clybourn Avenue
Chicago, Illinois 60614
FAX (312) 868-6250